Collected Prose

ROBERT HAYDEN

Foreword by William Meredith

Edited by Frederick Glaysher

Ann Arbor   The University of Michigan Press

D0944641

Library of Congress Cataloging in Publication Data

Hayden, Robert Earl, 1913–
   Collected prose.

   (Poets on poetry)
   1. Poetry—Addresses, essays, lectures.   I. Glaysher,
Frederick, 1954–   II. Title.   III. Series.
PS3515.A9363A6   1984   818′.5208   84-3602
ISBN 0-472-06351-0 (pbk.)

Collected
Prose

Poets on Poetry Donald Hall, General Editor

Foreword

Robert Hayden was a man as gifted in humanity as he was in poetry. His death in Ann Arbor, Michigan on February 25, 1980 struck a host of readers like a personal loss, and acquaintances felt it like friends. The several memorials I went to seemed as intimate as wakes—it was as though there were no ranks of friendship among those who had known him, no degrees of loss.

There can be no ranks either among those who want his work to be more widely known and more generally available. In assembling this collection of his prose, Frederick Glaysher has done something that all friends of Hayden's achievement must be grateful for. These works comprise a lovely and enduring miscellany which the poet himself might have been too reticent to put forth as a book. But they belong in company with the too-small, imperishable body of his poems. In their different ways, each of them is open and generous-minded like their author.

He was born in the poor section of Detroit called Paradise Valley, in 1913. The ironical name of this slum area may have provided one of his earliest insights into the wry poetry of his people. In any case, he invoked it near the end of his life in the title and subjects of a fine autobiographical sequence in *American Journal.* He went to public schools in Detroit and, as we read in "Some Remembrances" here, won a scholarship to Detroit City College. He went on to do graduate work at the University of Michigan, where he came to know W. H.

Auden—he says he "studied with" him, but that's not the term Auden used about a poet for whom he came to have a high regard. Both poets were to die too soon, at 67. Hayden published his first book at 27, in 1940.

After graduate school, he went to Nashville and taught for more than two decades at Fisk University. His final teaching years were at the University of Michigan. He left Ann Arbor for other posts twice, once to teach at Connecticut College for a semester, and again in 1976–78 to serve as Consultant in Poetry to the Library of Congress.

A man of natural dignity, Robert Hayden accepted the many honors that came to him in later years modestly, as he had accepted neglect for most of his life philosophically. Besides the Poetry Consultancy, these honors were to include the Grand Prize for Poetry at the First World Festival of Negro Arts in Dakar in 1976, the Fellowship of the Academy of American Poets, the Loines Award (first given to Robert Frost), and later membership in the American Academy and Institute of Arts and Letters, several honorary degrees, and an invitation to read at the Carter White House. Coming after years of remarkable writing and teaching this recognition gratified but did not perceptibly change him from the gentle, powerful, original, and solitary genius he had always been.

In the 1960s, Hayden declared himself, at considerable cost in popularity, an American poet rather than a black poet, when for a time there was posited an unreconcilable difference between the two roles. There is scarcely a line of his which is not identifiable as an experience of black America, but he would not relinquish the title of American writer for any narrower identity.

When he was in Providence in 1976 to receive an honorary degree from Brown University he told of an experience at Ann Arbor when he first went back there to teach. A young black man came to his office one day, not on literary business but to reproach him for his dress. "How can you, a black man, come to your office day after day wearing a suit like that, the uniform of your white oppressor?" Hayden was elegantly dressed that morning in Providence, when he told the story.

"I've always liked to dress myself up a little," he said then, "and I told this boy, 'I'm just coming into my style, boy. You ain't seen nothin' yet.'"

It was his work to share and enlighten the American black experience, not to diminish it by rancor. This he did by the difficult, simple method of almost flawless art, an art which finally called so loud across the chasm of race that, at last, he was heard on both sides, reminding us of our humanity. His is a complex vision of mutual responsibility. He maintained it optimistically, as he maintained his Bahá'í faith and his high personal code. In a famous poem called "The Whipping" he found an emblem for his compassion. The poem begins by appealing to our sense of terrible injustice, as we watch an old woman pursue and beat a young boy with uncontrollable rage. Then the woman's rage and ours subside as the speaker tells of whippings of his own childhood, "the blows, the fear worse than blows that hateful words could bring, the face that I no longer knew or loved." And then, miraculously, the poem melts with ruth:

> Well, it is over now, it is over,
>   and the boy sobs in his room,
>
> And the woman leans muttering against
>   a tree, exhausted, purged—
> avenged in part for lifelong hidings
>   she has had to bear.

I think it is this remarkable capacity for compassion which kept him from joining causes where anger took precedence over understanding. He understood but was committed to contend with Auden's dire pronouncement: "Those to whom evil is done / do evil in return," and his life and his work were attempts to break that cycle.

William Meredith
22 February 1983

Preface

Robert Hayden is now generally recognized as the most outstanding craftsman of Afro-American poetry. But too often such recognition fails to see deeper into the poems of Robert Hayden; too often it overlooks the fact that a large part of his poetry is on other than Afro-American themes. Like Yeats, who achieves universality through his commitment to, and exploration of, his Irish heritage, Hayden attains it through his dedication to his Afro-American background: humanity remains the subject. This is apparent in Hayden's poems as well as in the prose reprinted here.

The difficulty we face in our attempt to appreciate Hayden's work is that we are still provincial; we think too much in terms of nationality and race; we do not see or take seriously the value of a body of poetry that has as one of its major themes the inadequacy of such conceptions. He himself gave his vision its best expression; a vision which mankind, on this side of the globe as in the United States, indeed throughout the world, must continue to evolve toward:

> Reclaim now, now renew the vision of
> a human world where godliness
> is possible and man
> is neither gook nigger honkey wop nor kike
>
> but man
>
>   permitted to be man.

This emphasis on his universality is not intended to gainsay his allegiance to his heritage. It is merely to point out the importance of what he himself repeatedly, quietly said, as in one of the selections reprinted here: "As a Bahá'í I am committed to belief in the fundamental oneness of all races, the essential oneness of mankind, to the vision of world unity."

Thanks are due and appreciative acknowledgment made to the publishers and magazines credited on the first page of each selection for permission to reprint copyrighted material.

Maebashi, Japan: 1982

Contents

III. INTERVIEWS AND CONVERSATIONS

I

Addresses and
a Play

"How It Strikes a Contemporary"
Reflections on Poetry and the Role of the Poet

I call him the Inquisitor, though he is more like Chekhov's Black Monk than anything else. He has appeared in my study on several occasions—once or twice during the sixties and most recently a few weeks ago.

Each of his visits has been unannounced, if not entirely unexpected.

I cannot say that I wholly dislike the Inquisitor, though neither can I say that I enjoy his company. But his attitudes toward me and my work do have a stimulating effect, and, I have come to believe, an ultimately salutary influence. Nevertheless, I wonder sometimes if the remedy isn't worse than the disease. I can value him at certain moments as a sort of Reader over your Shoulder—to use Robert Graves's term. He often reminds me of the tough old woman I once knew who said to me, "Boy, what you messin' round with all that poetry stuff for? Ain't no percentage in *that*."

Quite often this Devil's Advocate looks and sounds like certain acquaintances of mine who feel it is their duty to see that I keep both feet on the ground. Or like certain professors I have endured who have tried in vain to convince me that Shakespeare said it all and therefore I should accept the fact

This dialogue was first delivered as an address at the Library of Congress on 8 May 1978 and is previously unpublished. Copyright © 1984 by Erma Hayden. Published with permission.

that I was born with too little too late. Yes, he is very similar at times to these self-appointed guardians of poetry. Not to mention his resemblance to certain "criticasters" for whom my blackness is so dense they can never see their way through or beyond it to me as a poet.

On his most recent visit, the Inquisitor seemed, I thought, more cynical and querulous than ever. But far less original. What he said then I have heard him say before. Most of his comments were simply repetitions of the misconceptions about poets and poetry current nowadays. And they brought out the unwilling didact in me.

I was writing when the Inquisitor entered the room. He seated himself on my worktable and began talking in his usual, peremptory fashion:

INQ.: Long time no see. How's the poetry business these days?

POET: You know how it irritates me to have you ask about "the poetry business."

INQ.: But it's such fun to needle you. All you poets take yourselves much too seriously. What're you writing?

POET: A talk I'm to give as my final performance at the Library of Congress. I'm having a hard time getting it into shape. I don't like lecturing anyway. I'm not good at it.

INQ.: Yes, I know. I've heard you.

POET: I'm not *that* bad.

INQ.: I've heard worse.

POET: Look here—I've more interesting things to do than listen to your snide remarks. Anyhow, we've been through something like this before.

INQ.: When did we last meet, by the way?

POET: During the late sixties. A couple of midnight sessions, as I recall.

INQ.: It was when you were trying to define the role of the poet in twentieth-century America—your own in particular; or some such nonsense. Did you succeed?

POET: I thought I had. But I've changed my mind since then, several times. I see the question differently now and rather feel that . . .

INQ.: Later, later. We'll get to your diatribe later, if you'll be so kind. Now this talk of yours . . .

POET: Just some of my own thoughts about poets and poetry.

INQ.: Well, you've always been one to take foolish risks. Got a title yet?

POET: Sure. "How It Strikes a Contemporary."

INQ.: Hey, ain't that from old Bob Browning?

POET: From *Robert* Browning, yes. One of my favorite poets, if you remember. I'm using the title of one of his poems. It's the one where he sees the poet as God's confidant:

> We had among us, not so much a spy,
> As a recording chief-inquistor,
> The town's true master if the town but knew!
> We merely kept a governor for form,
> While this man walked about and took account
> Of all thought, said and acted, then went home,
> And wrote it fully to our Lord the King. . . .

INQ.: Spare me. I've told you before I can't *stand* that old pious fraud. I consider him the Billy Sunday of English poetry—always grandstanding, always kidding himself that he's hitting home runs for Jesus or something.

POET: Oh, come off it. That's pretty silly, even for you. Anachronistic besides.

INQ.: You know what I mean. So now you're cribbing from Browning.

POET: Call it what you will. Twenty years ago you might have hurt me by saying that. But not now.

INQ.: I'm just getting warmed up. I guess you're feeling pretty feisty now because you've been Consultant in Poetry in Washington for a couple of years. Yes, I guess that would go to your head, wouldn't it? But tell me, what is it you do as Consultant—just prop your feet up on a desk and write deathless verse every day, or what?

POET: You *know* I never write with my feet propped up on a desk.

INQ.: You're not answering my question.

POET: I've heard it so many times that I'm sick and tired of answering it. I *consult,* what else?

INQ.: You've really got it made, if that's all you do.

POET: And that's plenty for a working poet, if you do it right. But to get on with this tedious discussion: I write letters, talk with visiting poets, take part in Library programs, give readings, talk to schoolchildren, and so on and so on. And in the time that's left, I sometimes have enough energy to work on my poems.

INQ.:   You've won some awards and stuff, haven't you?

POET: Yes, as if you didn't know.

INQ.:   Think you deserved them?

POET: Yes and no.

INQ.:   What do you mean, yes and no? Explain yourself.

POET: Never. You want me to have to give the money back—have the citations canceled?

INQ.:   You're forgetting something.

POET: And what's that?

INQ.:   You're black. A black poet. They wouldn't dare ask for their money back. That's why you got it in the first place.

POET: You just had to get that in, didn't you? You really are contemptible.

INQ.:   I'm a realist.

POET: You're a philistine, a bigot, a schlemiel.

INQ.:   You know I'm right. You're a token.

POET: Of what?

INQ.:   Somebody's bad conscience.

POET: Now listen, Buster, why don't you just get out of here?

INQ.: You can't make me. You know you can't get rid of me until I choose to leave. Remember last time when I made you so mad? Now that I've hit a nerve I'm going to stay here and enjoy seeing you squirm.

POET: Don't count on it. I've heard this kind of blather a good many times by now, and I shouldn't react to it, but I guess I always do. I'm old enough to know there's no defense against mean-spirited ignorance except to keep away from it. I know that but still react. You're implying that standards are different for me from what they are for other American poets. You're saying I must be granted considerations not on the basis of my work, but purely in terms of racial quotas, politics, and sociology.

INQ.: Well, not entirely, maybe. But you will admit, won't you, that people are less interested in you as a poet than as a *black poet*?

POET: Yes, I have reason to believe that's partly true—and true on *both* sides of the American color line today. But it's not *my* problem—my problem is to go on trying to be the poet I think I may some day become.

INQ.: But, look, you can't just ignore the social context— the, er, social situation your people are in. Don't you feel any responsibility toward *them*?

POET: You know very well, if you know anything about me at all, that I do, that I'm fully conscious, and sometimes painfully conscious, of their and my situation. But I assert my right to approach it in my own way as a poet. I deal with it as I feel it, and not as people like you think I should. After all, as a poet I am trying to come to grips with reality, yes, to define reality, as I can perceive it. Isn't that what every poet worthy of the name is attempting to do? Why does a particular racial identity make me any the less aware of life, life as human beings live it? What is a poet but a human being speaking to other human beings about things that matter to all of us? And of course some of these concerns are social and political—racial or ethnic, to use a currently fashionable word. But there are other matters that are also important. Sermons in stones—that sort of thing. To put it succinctly, I feel that Afro-American poets ought to be looked at as poets first, if that's what they truly are. And as one of them I dare to hope that if my work means anything, if it's any good at all, it's going to have a human impact, not a narrowly racial or ethnic or political and overspecialized impact. But, as Fats Waller said for all time, "One never *know, do* one?"

INQ.:   You always put too much importance on poetry. All you verse-makers do. Wasn't it Oscar Wilde who said that all art is quite useless?

POET: I think it was. And then W. H. Auden wrote in his elegy on Yeats that poetry makes nothing happen. I disagree with both points of view.

INQ.:   So what else is new? I recall your having some inflated notions about poetry being a spiritual act. And you once argued that a poet was a kind of priest— was at least the conscience of his culture. To all of which I say nonsense. Poets are just guys or dames who sit around playing with words like kids with brightly colored building blocks. They fool around long enough, they make something that looks like a poem. And poems are nothing but artifacts like blocks or chairs.

POET: And for the sake of argument, let us say that chairs are useful, aren't they? And necessary and sometimes beautiful.

INQ.: This is taking a funny turn. But, *touché, touché.*

POET: You're giving in? It's not like you.

INQ.: Twinges. I'm not myself tonight. I'm getting old. And so are you, incidentally.

POET: You recall Browning's lines: "Grow old along with me; / The best is yet to be. . . ."

INQ.: Oh, please, no more, no more. Sententious doggerel of a pompous old burgher. Let's get back to the subject. I was saying poetry is . . .

POET: You can't define it any better than I can. But I would make so bold as to say it's probably best defined by the poems a poet writes. For me that's the most fruitful attempt at a definition. Actually, I'd much rather spend my time writing poetry than worrying over what it is or isn't. A matter of feeling anyway, a matter of sensibility. I haven't much patience, hardly any in fact, with theories of poetry. They're all *after* the fact. It's the practice that gives rise to theory anyway, wouldn't you agree, however grudgingly?

INQ.: I'm sure I wouldn't. Does it matter whether I do or not?

POET: No.

At this point, the Inquisitor left abruptly. I was glad to be rid of him. Still, though he had angered and disconcerted me, as he usually does, he had also left me with some ideas that might be developed for my talk, even if only in a negative way. I took some scratch paper and scrawled several pages of notes:

1. *The nature and function of poetry:* Poetry as the illumination of experience through language. (The Inquisitor would surely accuse me of cribbing again; this time from Virginia Woolf, etc.) Poetry has always dealt with fundamental human concerns. Could we think of it as a species of Primal Scream? Did it not grow out of primitive mysteries? And does it not remain, despite all we know about it, rather mysterious?

2. *Poetry as a medium, an instrument for social and political change:* Poetry *does* make something happen, for it changes sensibility. In the early stages of a culture it helps to crystallize language and is a repository for value, belief, ideals. The *Griot* in African tribes keeps names and legends and pride alive. Among the Eskimos the shaman or medicine man is a poet. In ancient Ireland and Wales the bard was a preserver of the culture. Academicians and purists to the contrary notwithstanding, great poets of the past as well as the present have often been spokesmen for a cause, have been politically involved. A point to consider: What would I as a poet do if my people were rounded up like the Jewish people in Germany under the Nazis? Claude McKay's sonnet "If We Must Die"; the poems of the Greek poet Yannis Ritsos that were recited and sung by men and women fighting in the streets for the freedom of their country; Pablo Neruda, William Butler Yeats, Emily Sachs, Muriel Rukeyser, Gwendolyn Brooks, Walt Whitman; they stand out as poets even if you dislike their politics. To be a poet, it seems to me, is to care passionately about justice and one's fellow beings. Sometimes this is not true. Ezra Pound, for instance. Also note that much political or protest or socially conscious poetry is bad, not because of the poet's loyalties or affiliations but owing to lack of talent; sometimes to a pragmatist's contempt for art as a means of understanding and grace.

3. *Poetry as therapy:* A great many people are writing poetry today—I do not call them poets—who are not so much concerned with art or craft as they are with achieving some kind of emotional or psychic release. I'm sure this is good for them, and there is no questioning the therapeutic value of poetry, of the arts in general. But if therapy is all one is after I hardly consider it justifies one considering himself a poet. But of course they do. They are, I am well aware, often seeking escape from the anonymity that threatens us all. They are seeking affirmation of their being, their uniqueness, through poetry or other forms of art. But self-expression becomes an end in itself; questions of craftsmanship, form, style are likely to be dismissed as "elitist" and therefore irrelevant. I would not object to the self-expressionists but for the fact that their efforts result in delusions of poetic grandeur. When I discussed Mr. X's poetry with him in the Poetry Office one day, I soon recognized him as the counterpart of Miss Y, who invaded my office at the University of Michigan with a sheaf of mediocre verses—all terribly *fraught,* as an old friend used to say of such efforts. Both would-be poets were visibly annoyed when I pointed out weaknesses in diction, imagery, *and* grammar, because they thought these things of minor consequence, since the poems expressed their feelings. And, oh, the sine qua non of all sine qua nons: their poems were *spontaneous* (not labored over like yours, sir). "No, I never rewrite my poems; I let them come as they will and do not revise. I've been writing for about a year, and all my friends are after me to publish a book. Tell me how to get my work published."

   Well, you do what you can with these hopeless cases. You send up a silent prayer that time and hard-nosed poetry editors will show these people the error of their ways.

4. *Poetry as the art of saying what cannot be said or at least not said quite so effectively in any other form:* Maybe I've worn this statement out, I've used it so many times, and should give it a long rest. But somehow I can't resist repeating it. What

I have said in my poems I am sure I could not otherwise have said. Indeed, I might have said too much. A poem is built on silences as well as on sounds. And it imposes a silence audible as a laugh, a sigh, a groan.

A few nights ago, I was looking over these notes and wondering how on earth I'd work them into the talk when the Inquisitor arrived. Shall I pretend I was not glad for the interruption?

INQ.:   I know why I've been so groggy lately that I let you get the better of the argument sometimes. I know what's wrong, yesiree.

POET: Then tell me. The suspense is unbearable.

INQ.:   I'm tired of poets and poetry, worn out by all the rapping I've had to endure regarding the role of the poet, the function of poetry in this society.

POET: You're one of the chief instigators. And you've never been exactly our friend. You've always . . .

INQ.:   Don't interrupt. All this palavering about the American poet's role. What else is it but to be a poet and write verses? A useless function at best, but never mind. You don't hear electricians and plumbers bellyaching the way you versifiers do.

POET: They've got unions.

INQ.:   Well, your crowd has too, in a manner of speaking; you're all professors nowadays, most of you at any rate. You're all safely inside the ivy-covered walls of Academe, grousing, or as you say when you're being cute, *kvetching*. No two ways about it, you're a sorry bunch. All you characters calling yourselves poets, oh, but playing it safe, observing the rules, conforming to what is expected of you as responsible citizens. Baudelaire and Rimbaud would laugh their heads off if they could see you. You and your faculty club teas, your polite conversation and mildly vicious gossip. No passion, no wildness, no risking anything. What a bunch of phonies you are. And, oh, those carefully contrived little poems you write about life in outer suburbia.

POET: Stop it already. Why don't you say something original for a change, even if you can't distinguish between truth and appearances. You're stereotyping us because you're intellectually too lazy to be discriminating. I grant you that the university is not necessarily the best environment for poets, because energies that should go into creative work too often are dissipated by routine and academic drudgery of one kind or another. Still, it's less enervating than picking cotton or working in a factory. And I guess as teachers we must be making some contribution to students, giving them what they couldn't get from anyone else. Few of us, and it's a very small few, earn enough from our books and our poetry readings to live on. So we have to do the impossible and somehow manage as best we can to pursue what are really two full-time jobs, two demanding careers.

INQ.: Careers, careers! You poets today think too much about your careers. You're so busy being seen by the right people at the right time in the right place, you're so greedy for publicity and fame, you're so busy promoting yourselves I wonder that you ever find time to do what poets are supposed to do—write poems. I'm fed up with the whole flipping lot of you. Nothing but hustlers.

POET: If we are, it's because of you and your crowd.

INQ.:   Let your poems do the hustling.

POET: And let your fingers do the walking, I suppose.

INQ.:   That's clever, that is. I'll die laughing.

POET: Let your poems do the hustling, indeed!

INQ.:   That's what I said. Worry about writing well. That's all that's important.

POET: As if you gave a tinker's dam about poetry. You're only saying it because you know it gets me worked up. And you'll be telling me next to live in a garret and go hungry so's to produce a masterpiece.

INQ.:   Why don't some of you birds give it a try?

POET: Because we're none of us characters in *La Bohème*. And because some of us know what real poverty is. Food and shelter and a few amenities have never prevented a real poet from writing real poetry.

INQ.:   Enough of this blather. I told you I'm tired of talking about poetry.

POET: Well, you started it, Buster, and I'm not going to let you have the last word. You flout the value, the importance of poetry and you heap ridicule on poets. But there are thousands tonight who except for us would have no one to speak in a human voice for them. Who more earnestly than poets have warned of the dangers of abstraction and anonymity to the human spirit?

INQ.:   He's off and running.

POET: Let there be poets and more poets—just as long as they are poets. For poets too are the keepers of a nation's conscience, the partisans of freedom and justice, even when they eschew political involvement. By the very act of continuing to function as poets they are affirming what is human and eternal. And as I have contemplated the almost bewildering diversity of American poetry, I have come to see a vital relationship between the poetic endeavor and freedom of speech in this country. In the monolithic dictatorships poets are silenced unless they repeat the clichés of the state. The dangers of censorship in our own country are certainly present, and although I would not overstate the case by saying it is poets who are chiefly keeping the lines of verbal communication open, I will say that we know the dangers of censorship and we are therefore part of the advance guard in the struggle. When poets are silenced then tyranny has won.

Well, maybe the Inquisitor did have the last word, for he disappeared while I was still talking. It was quite late, way past midnight, and I was exhausted, but I stayed up to make a few notes. I wouldn't have slept even if I had gone to bed, because I was thinking of all the things I should have said to that old curmudgeon but had not had the presence of mind or sufficient wit to say. I reached for a notebook and scribbled some of them down. Perhaps I could use them in my talk.

From *The Life*
Some Remembrances

On an icy afternoon last January the poet walked for the first time in many years through the old Detroit neighborhood where he was born and raised. He moved somewhat uncertainly in the cold bleak light, a little self-consciously, for his walk was being filmed by a TV camera crew for scenes in a documentary. "So I have become a grey eminence," he thought wryly. "But not, I hope, a good grey poet." As he moved down Beacon Street, the director asked him to point out the spot where the house the poet was born in had stood. A warehouse stands there now. On the opposite side of the street, a parking lot and a power plant have replaced the house his family occupied until he was ten or eleven years old. The only familiar object remaining there is the street lamp that used to shine through the lace curtains at the bay window of the front room. That front room with its wide brass bed, its gasolier shedding a soft lemon light, its family portraits in heavy baroque frames—a room where Christmas trees as well as coffins had stood.

A street lamp. A point of reference. Hattie and Elmer and

This chapter from Hayden's intended autobiography was first delivered as an address at the Library of Congress on 3 May 1977 and is previously unpublished. This chapter is the only one that Hayden wrote. Copyright © 1984 by Erma Havden. Published with permission.

M. C. the tomboy who died in her teens, and he, old Four-Eyes, playing hide-and-seek on summer nights and one-two-three red light, touching the lamp post and shouting "Free! Free!"

Summer evening time. It is always summer when he thinks of his life on Beacon Street. The grownups sit on the front porch, taking their ease after the demands and vexations of the day. Leaf shadows of trees of heaven. Ma is smoking Piedmont cigarettes. Pa is nodding. Auntie is taking the cool, as people used to say, before she goes to the Chinese restaurant where she is a waitress.

The waffle wagon, its bells tinkling, approaches. "Pa, can I have a nickel to buy a waffle?" The crab man, his steamer filled with shrimp and crabs, passes, calling out in a high thin voice, "Crab man. Steamin'. Crab man." Down on the corner a preacher and two stout women with tambourines begin singing a Baptist hymn. It is long-metered, filled with a lugubrious hope. Afterward, the preacher delivers a sermon—hell-fire and damnation and brimstone. A small crowd has gathered around him. "Ma, can I go down to the corner, can I, Ma, please?" It is the tambourines that attract the children, not the preacher, but the tambourines and the singing, for what the preacher says is scary. When the women pass through the crowd with the preacher's hat asking for money for their church, the sinner men and women drop in a coin or two in expiation of their sins.

The poet moved with the director and the camera crew up Beacon Street to St. Antoine, the principal and notorious street in Paradise Valley. Paradise Valley, that ironically named area of the old east side ghetto. St. Antoine: Saint Anthony: pronounced by Detroiters St. Anto-wine. Detroit's Beale Street. Respectable people shunned it as the devil's. It was often described as a sort of crossroads of the "colored world." "You stand on St. Antoine and sooner or later everbody you know or ever heard of will be passing by."

St. Antoine. Kaleidoscopic in memory now, its sordidness all but forgotten. Restaurants, barbershops, pool halls, cabarets, blind pigs, gamblin' joints camouflaged as "Recreation

Clubs." Shootings, stabbings, blaring jazz, and a liveliness, a gaiety at once desperate and releasing, at once wicked—Satan's playground—and good-hearted.

You might see Jack Johnson in the latter days of his flamboyant glory, Ethel Waters or Bessie Smith, the blues singers, between shows at the old Koppin Theater, and Tiger Flowers and Kid Chocolate, and later Joe Louis.

And there were parades. In the hot sunshine of a Sunday afternoon the followers of Marcus Garvey, storm center of the Back to Africa movement (United Negro Improvement Association) during the 1920s, might be seen there marching in purple and green, carrying banners with black stars on them; chevaliers with plumed hats, black star nurses, children in trucks festooned with crepe paper. People stood along the curb watching, outraged or reassured. "Damn fools," one man might say. "I sure ain't lost nothing in Africa and I'm sure as hell ain't going there to look for nothing." "Just like a zigaboo to talk like that," another might say. "Garvey trying to bring our race together and here you are low-rating him. Man, he talks good sense. We the onlies nation in the world don't have a country of our own and don't have a flag of our own."

But nobody quarreled when the Colored Elks or the Colored Masons or Woodmen stepped it off along St. Antoine. The music, the precision of the drill teams, the polish and gleam and sparkle, the ribbons and badges. Ethiopia spreading her gorgeous wings.

And Hallowe'en there took on something of the color and spirit of Mardi Gras. The poet recalls how he and the other children would dress up in their elders' stale-sweet clothes, put on masks bought for a few cents from the candy store, and become the unknown beings that in their unshared minds they knew they were. They were allowed to go from house to house in the early part of the evening, to roam the streets to mystify. It seems not to have been the custom in Detroit in those days to threaten with the cry of "Trick or Treat." He had no recollection of ever doing this. Sometimes they would draw pictures on windows or smear them with soap. But mostly they walked around in their false faces, white sheets and long skirts dragging, old pants whose bagginess and patches were part of the fun. The poet always hoped nobody knew who he was, but the thick glasses made it hard for him to wear the mask so that his face was completely hidden.

Later, the children would go with their parents to watch the grown-up masqueraders make their surreal progress along St. Antoine. Clowns, red devils with curling tails, Zulus, men in evening gowns, women in tuxedos, each sex a parody of the other. The poet often thought of this scene when reading Rimbaud's strangely reverberating Parade: "*J'ai seul le clef a cette parade sauvage.*" And he remembers how some of the masqueraders would frighten the children, approaching them with menacing gestures. The parade of outlandish creatures lasted for several hours and ended as abruptly as it had begun. The parents took the children home to bed.

But nobody was on the streets of Paradise Valley that cold afternoon. And other than a few buildings he did not remember having seen before there was little here to attract attention. The camera crew took a few more pictures, then they all drove up a few blocks to where he had lived while a student at Detroit City College, now Wayne State University. Here too, not much of the original scene was left, most of the houses and other buildings having been torn down.

For the poet this was no sentimental trek back into the past. He felt no nostalgia, no longing for the good old days, perhaps in this respect disappointing the young TV men. No, he was not going to play the old codger with golden memories. He knew that the good old days in the Detroit slums had never been good. Actually, he might have reacted somewhat differently, responded more emotionally, if he had not exteriorized, objectified for himself his feelings about the area and the life he had lived there in a series of poems written the year before—"Elegies for Paradise Valley." He used the name to designate the entire ghetto, not just the segment of it he had just traversed. How well he knew this part of the town, having spent twenty-seven years of his life there, moving always, as he liked to say, from one dilapidated house to another. Still, these streets recalled for him voices, faces he had loved and whose loss even now, after how many years—close to forty maybe—he mourned. A way of life forever a part of his consciousness as an artist, forever a source for his poems, and forever a source of joy and pain never to be assuaged by awards, published books, prestige, accomplishment, such as it was, nor by the security that had come to him in the latter years of his life—a security distrusted and perhaps even feared.

No, this was no nostalgia "trip" for him. He felt today no sadness, no regret, remembering things past. These were all in the poem, and poems for him were often a means of catharsis, a way, he often thought, of gazing upon the Medusa without being turned to stone, the poem being his mirror shield. Anyway, he was a survivor. He had broken through somehow. By force of a talent he had, but again, often doubted, often mistrusted? Was it luck that had enabled him to make the long and surprising journey from Paradise Valley to the Library of Congress? Pa had often told him, "Get something in your head and they can't take it away from you. Stay in school, don't let me catch you hanging around in the streets. I don't want you to live like I've had to live. You don't have to live like this. Go to school." Was it education, then? But he felt himself an ignorant fool mostly. Was it sheer luck? "Boy, you look so much like your mama, and a boy that look like his mama the way you do is born for luck."

He had escaped the slum life he had hated so vehemently after he went to college. Yet he remained loyal in many respects to what he called the "folk." He often spoke with a certain smugness of having grown up in the slums, of having been spared little of the squalor and ugliness and humiliations that largely characterized that life. Yes, he rather enjoyed the discomfiture of middle-class acquaintances who considered such talk in bad taste, a sort of gratuitous insult to them. His early years as the foster son of poor working-class people, the conflicts between them and his own natural parents left him with a deep ambivalence toward life and a sense of alienation nothing could alter. They must also account for the persona who recurs in some of his poems, The Stranger, as well as for certain themes and a predilection for the folk idiom.

Not too long ago, he decided to include as part of the design of a new series of poems words and phrases remembered from childhood and youth. Under the title of *Gumbo Ya Ya*—Creole patois for "Everybody talks"—he wrote down several pages, hoping of course, to make use of them in poems later on. Here are a few selections:

1. God don't like ugly and cares damn little for beauty.
2. She looks like a picture done fell out the frame.
3. Goodbye. Sweet potato, plant you now and dig you later.
4. Every shut-eye ain't sleep and every goodbye ain't gone.
5. Married? The man ain't born and his mother's dead.
6. He's a bigger liar than old Tom Culpepper and you know the devil kicked him out of hell nine times before breakfast for lying.
7. Yez, Lawd, I got me three changes a day—in rags, outa rags, and no damn rags a-tall.
8. I promised God and nine other men I wouldn't do that again.
9. Gonna hit you so hard your coattail will fly up like a window shade.
10. To be a good liar you got to have a good remembrance.

As a child he was considered rather precocious. "An old man's head on a boy's shoulders." He learned to read before entering school and he began trying to write plays and stories and poems while still in the grades. He remembers that he once wrote a story about Anna Pavlova, the ballerina whose pictures he had seen on posters outside Orchestra Hall, thus fulfilling the assignment to make sentences using the words in the spelling manual.

Although there were few books in his home, he borrowed books from the public library and occasionally received books as gifts from members of the family. Nearsighted all his life, he was sent to what was called the Sight-Saving room when he entered junior high and his teachers forbade him to read small print. This of course made books all the more attractive, since he was forbidden to read them.

By the time he entered high school he had discovered poetry and had begun the arduous and obsessive task of becoming a poet. He read Countee Cullen and Langston Hughes, Carl Sandburg and Edna St. Vincent Millay. He began to try to describe the life around him, taking his clues from Sandburg and Hughes.

During the depression of the thirties, his family had to go on welfare, and he would remember for the rest of his life the feelings of guilt and shame they experienced. To be poor, it seemed, was to be considered immoral or at least inherently inferior and congenitally shiftless because we were, after all, Afro-American. We tried to conceal the fact that we were on the dole. But of course there were a few defiant souls among us who declared, "They ain't givin' us nothin' except what we got coming to us by rights. Hell, ain't we worked for it?" But this was of no comfort to those like Pa for whom work, however hard, was as necessary to his well-being as religion was.

One day, the poet remembers, he was sent to the welfare station to bring home the sack of potatoes or flour or whatever was being distributed to the welfare clients. He took his place in the line and began reading a book he had brought with him. "Always got his head stuck in a book," Ma used to say in irritation. Around him, the others, in their ill-smelling clothes smelling of bacon grease and sweat and hair oil, joshed and laughed with one another or compared notes on the meanness of the caseworkers. Most of the caseworkers were hated by their clients, for many of them were racist in their attitude. And most of the people waiting in the line would have agreed that the black caseworkers were worse than the white, perhaps because they were ashamed of their own people, or perhaps because they were trying to prove to their superiors that they could be as tough and impartial toward the members of their own race as anyone else could. There were exceptions, of course. As the poet stood reading—it was Cullen's first book of poems, *Color*, he recalls—

reading half-heartedly and hoping that no one he knew would see him standing there, the worker in charge of his family happened to come out of her office. He disliked her intensely but tried not to show it. She smiled at him and asked, "What's that you're reading?" "A book of poems by Countee Cullen," he replied. "He is a great Negro poet, you know, and some day I am going to have a book published too." She made some casual remark like "That's nice" and turned away.

Several days later when the worker came to the house she gave him the name of a man who might be able to help him get a tuition scholarship to Detroit City College through the State Rehabilitation Service. "If you're going to be a poet you ought to get a good education," she offered.

It sounds like the plot of a grade-B movie. The official to whom the poet went was a merry little Scots-Irishman whose face and voice the poet has remembered ever since. After a brief interview, the eyes sizing up the nervous thick-spectacled would-be poet before him, he exclaimed, "Of course, you're going to college, if I have anything to say in the matter!" And in the fall of that year, the poet, the scared, hopeful, bedeviled boy from a family none of whose members had ever finished grade school, became a freshman at Detroit City College.

He received relatively little encouragement as a poet at first. One instructor to whom he showed his poems hinted that he might better spend his time elsewhere, since he clearly did not have the makings of a poet. The effect of this judgment was devastating and long-lasting. As a teacher of creative writing himself now, he never tells a student poet he is hopeless. And if a student asks directly, "Do you think I ought to go on? Do you think I am a poet?" he will reply, "That is something you will find out for yourself. I assure you the time will come when you'll know whether you should go on or not. If poetry nags at you, if it's something you feel incomplete without, then you'll go on because you'll have to. One cannot learn to be a poet. One is born a poet. One does not choose this art but is chosen by it. And, finally, it is a gift, something given, and if you are to be worthy to receive it you must give everything you are in return."

As a young poet, poetry was for him no doubt an escape, a release. It was a way of discovery, discovery of self and the world. It was the magic power of words. It was too, he often thought when older, the exorcism of personal demons who must leave the spirit when their tormented unwilling host learns to say their names. Words. Names. Ah, yes, he knew their power to hurt or heal. Nigger. Four-Eyes, sissy.

In college he met other young poets and often exchanged poems with them. A few of his poems began to appear in the campus paper as well as in the Afro-American weeklies published in Detroit. This period he afterward described as his socially conscious period. At Detroit City College he was in touch with the young radicals, though he was always less interested in politics than in what we now refer to as the humanities. Nevertheless, he, like so many other poets of the time, wrote poems protesting the injustice of the Scottsboro Boys trial. He took part in antiwar rallies and wrote what he hoped were searing lyrical indictments of the cruelty and absurdity of war. Venturing to read his poems for the members of the John Reed Club, he was scathingly criticized for his lack of political awareness. And he was often accused of being too much the individualist and not willing to submit to ideology. (He heard these same words spoken by one of the militant leaders of the sixties and left the meeting at which the speaker appeared, saying, "This is where I came in thirty years ago.")

There is a great deal of talk today, much of it generating more heat than light, about black identity. Our poet, now something of an old curmudgeon, is likely to be heard protesting that he doesn't understand what all the fuss is about. "I always knew who and what I was," he has said. "Remember, I grew up in the ghetto, which, if mixed in those days, was predominantly Afro-American. I never had any trouble relating to the people around me. There was, of course, color prejudice among us—the dark-skinned with 'bad' or what we call today 'natural' hair, and the fair-skinned or the light brown with 'good' hair. My own family exhibited several shades and gradations of pigmentation. But I never thought of the people I knew as being anything but human. My playmates were, for a time, Italian, Jewish, even Southern white, for the old neighborhood had in the first years of the century been settled by people of several different ethnic backgrounds. I ate halvah and smoked fish in the homes of the Jewish kids; I went to school with Italians and Greeks and Poles. At the age of twelve or thirteen I even knew a few words of Chinese, because Kuni, the son of the owner of the Chinese restaurant where my aunt worked for so many years off and on, and I were friends and went to the Detroit Institute of Musical Arts together for violin lessons. As far as the members of my own race were concerned, I loved or disliked them purely on the basis of their pleasing or displeasing actions and personalities.

"I find it touching to recall that when it became known I would be entering college, many people came to tell me how proud they were and pressed a quarter or a fifty-cent piece or a dollar in my hand.

"In the late thirties I wrote a poem which I called a mass chant, 'These Are My People.' I try never to write poems I do not myself believe in."

After college, the poet was fortunate enough to get a job on the Federal Writers Project—the WPA. Nearly all the young writers he had known at Wayne were on the project.

But we have left the poet and the TV crew out in the cold long enough. It's time we let them get into the car and drive first to the old Second Baptist Church, where the poet and his foster father were members in more or less good standing. The church has been designated a historical landmark by the state of Michigan, and when the documentary is released the poet will be shown reading the gold-lettered plaque outside. Second Baptist is the *mise en scène* for his poem, "Mourning Poem for the Queen of Sunday."

Leaving Second Baptist, the poet returned with the others to the luxurious suite at a posh hotel provided him and his wife by an organization that would present him with a distinguished citizen award.

He said to the TV men over coffee in the room: "Please don't take pictures of me in this room. Or at least, don't show me sitting at that French Provincial table surrounded by all this luxury. It hardly seems appropriate to the kind of poetry I write. And, besides, I am still something of a Calvinist. All Americans, black or white, are Calvinist, you know, whatever their professed religious faith may be."

There followed a series of questions about the poet's work, his philosophy, the effect of the Bahá'í Faith upon his work. "I saw very little influence on my work for the first several years," he told them, "but now I realize it has given me a base, a focus. I am not very pious, certainly not in any sense a goody-goody. Indeed, I still struggle with my faith; it harrows up my soul, as I guess it is supposed to do. And I confess that as an artist I find it extremely difficult to conform to the letter of the law. But I have learned from it that the work of the artist, the scientist, the philosopher, all sincere effort in any discipline has spiritual value and is both a form of service and a form of worship. This thought sustains me when the dark times come, and they come for me all too often, I must admit.

"Once I might have thought of poetry as a release from tension, as catharsis, which it sometimes surely is. And once the writing of a poem might have provided me an escape from the ugliness I had to endure—the spiritual ugliness, let me say. But now I think of poetry—of my own poetry—as a way of coming to grips with reality, as a way of discovery and definition. It is a way of solving for the unknowns. And, yes, it is something bigger and simpler and more complex than any of these things."

At last the cameramen packed up their gear and left with the director.

"I wonder if I said the right things today," the poet thought. "After all these years I still don't know what I'm talking about when it comes to poetry. I'm never going to let myself be interviewed again."

But he would have to find time to see the reporter from the *Detroit News* who wanted to interview him tomorrow morning.

The History of Punchinello

A Baroque Play in One Act

CHARACTERS:

The Comedian	The Puppet
The Dancer	The Manager
The Porter	The Producer
The Tragedian Image	Three Masked Figures

The action of the play takes place in the Comedian's dressing room in a New York theatre on a night in the early 1920s.

The room is simple, unattractive, containing a dressing table with lighted mirror, two chairs, a clothes-tree on which the street clothes of the Comedian are hung. The one unusual object in the dressing room is a tall mirror, its frame heavily gilded and ornamented in baroque style.

At the height of the laughter and the applause, the Comedian enters the dressing room. He wears a full blackface mask on which a grotesque red-lipped smile has been painted, an ill-fitting frock coat sewn with huge sunflowers, too-big white cotton workman's gloves, a battered top hat. He carries a cane with gaudy ribbons.

The Comedian goes to the dressing table with the offstage noises loud in his ears; gazes at his reflection in the dressing table mirror, then crosses to the door and slams it shut with an oath of disgust. He

From *SADSA Encore* (Nashville: Fisk University, 1948), pp. 30–33. Written about the comedian Bert Williams. Performed by the Department of Drama at Fisk University during the late 1940s.

throws the cane aside, takes off the hat, tears off the mask, flinging
them onto the table. He takes a few turns about the room. By now the
sounds offstage have completely subsided.

COMEDIAN

Black doll. Coonjine jester
buckdancing to a jangle of laughter: That's
me. Jack in the box. Jump, Jack.
Sambo puppet on a string. What else, what else?

The Dancer enters, happy and excited. Her costume is a sort of
ballet dress, sewn like the Comedian's, with large sunflowers, and she
wears these flowers in her hair.

DANCER

Oh darling, you were marvelous,
so unpredictable, so clever. (*She kisses him.*)

COMEDIAN

Thank you, my dear . . . for the kiss.

DANCER

And have you ever, ever
heard such laughter, such applause!

COMEDIAN

I hate their laughter.

DANCER

All sense of guilt and strife
dissolved, became unreal, illusive after
you appeared. Giving them laughter
you give the people life.

COMEDIAN

And what do they give me, and to the people
I symbolize for them, what do they give?
What but death, but death?

DANCER

I see you've grown morose again.
This is your first success, don't brood,
don't poke and pry; accept it and.be glad.

COMEDIAN

But when I think, oh when I think of all
that I could do . . . and of the little I'm allowed to do.
Well, they say the puppet comes in time
to love his strings, the jack his box.

Accept the mad teaparty, it's not so bad,
but you're a true comedian, my longfaced lad,
that's why you're always moping, sad.

*There is a knock at the door. The Dancer opens it, and the Porter
enters with a large basket of flowers, long-stemmed roses predomi-
nating.*

DANCER

Oh, how beautiful!

PORTER

From your admirers, sir.
If you'll permit me, sir, I thought that you
were wonderfully comical tonight.
I stood backstage and laughed and laughed and laughed.

*The Comedian acknowledges this with a slight but gracious bow.
The Porter sets the basket down, goes out.*

DANCER

You see, my dear, you see
what your public thinks of you!
The time is coming when there'll be no two-
a-day for you, when there will be
a big star on your door;
that's what I deeply wish for, hope for.

COMEDIAN

It's wonderful of you to care so much. Wear these
for me tonight. (*He reaches for the roses and
brings his hand back sharply*) They're full of thorns, like all
their gifts to me. Take these instead. (*Gives her
some of the others.*)

DANCER

They're lovely. Thank you, dear. I'll run
and change now. Wait for me downstairs.
And have a big smile ready for me.

*She kisses him and goes out. Left alone, the Comedian takes a few
steps about the room, deep in thought. At length he returns to the
dressing table, begins to change. He stops and picks up the mask, runs
his fingers over it, laughs wryly. He slips it on a moment, sits looking
into the dressing table mirror.*

COMEDIAN
(playing a role)
Who dar? What dat? When
is ah'm gonna ain't? Bengal tigers
in de moonlight. Bigfoot shadders
stalkin'. When dat dead man raises up
in de chilly moonlight and turns his eye
on me, why, they're gonna be a do'
whar they wasn't none befo.'

He takes off the mask, wearily tosses it aside; takes off the sunflower coat. In the process of changing to street clothes he goes over to the large mirror. As he stands there he imagines himself in the role of a Shakespearian Tragedian.

The Tragedian Image appears in the mirror. As he recites from Shakespeare's Richard the Second *the Image follows his gestures.*

COMEDIAN

For God's sake, let us sit upon the ground
And tell sad stories of the death of kings:
How some have been deposed; some slain in war;
Some haunted by the ghosts they have deposed:
Some poison'd by their wives; some sleeping kill'd;
All murder'd: for within the hollow crown
That rounds the mortal temples of a king
Keeps Death his court and there the antic sits,
Scoffing his state and grinning at his pomp. . . .

He moves away from the mirror, the Tragedian Image receding as the Comedian comes downstage.

COMEDIAN

No use. No use. I am the coonjine doll
with guts of straw and watermelon grin.
My gilded cowardice, fantastic sidlings,
extravagant sloth are gaudy offerings
to appease and flatter them, since I must act
or die, the limelight circles of the stage
the only country where I freely breathe.

He crosses to dressing table and sits down as he soliloquizes. The full-length mirror lights up: it is a puppet booth now. In it appears a marionette of the Comedian, dressed exactly as the Comedian was when he first came into the dressing room. The Puppet dances and grimaces grotesquely as the Comedian speaks.

COMEDIAN

Night after night they come to laugh at me
and do not understand or won't admit
I am themselves. What are my monkeyshines
in the haunted house, the black infested grove
but exorcism of their own dark ghosts,
but their own fears made small and bearable?
They see me and learn nothing. Oh, I tire
of their empty laughter, being one who finds
more to lament than laugh at in this world
and knowing man, whatever else he thinks
himself to be, is tragic—a creature of
flawed magnificence and marvelous
despairs, who knows that to be perfect is
to die yet is so moulded he must try
to reach perfection; who yearns to be a god
and in the attempt becomes a raving devil.
Oh, these are things Marlowe and Shakespeare knew,
and these are things I long most passionately
to say. How glorious to speak them through
Prince Hamlet, who is youth confronted by
the evils and the dread alternatives
of life subservient to death. And huge
Macbeth, ambition run to madness, ruin,
such as we see in these our bloodied times.
And lordly Othello, noble and betrayed
by his nobility. But no, but no,
They will not have me. . . .

There is a knock at the door. The Puppet show disappears.

COMEDIAN

Come in.

The Manager and the Fabulous Producer enter. They are hard, flashy men.

MANAGER

I've brought someone who'd like to talk to you.

COMEDIAN

I'm very tired, gentlemen; couldn't we . . .

PRODUCER

Congratulations on your act. Uproariously funny.
Real darkey stuff. Oh, so that's how you look
beneath the getup, eh? I'd never guess.

COMEDIAN

Almost human, am I not?

MANAGER

I think you'll find it worth your time to be civil
to this gentleman. You may have heard of him,
the Fabulous Producer.

COMEDIAN

I'm glad to meet you, sir. Won't you sit down?

PRODUCER

Thank you. (*Sits down.*)

MANAGER

The Fabulous Producer here has a new sensational
sparkling big revue rehearsing at this very moment
and . . .

PRODUCER

I have an absolutely captivating part for you.

COMEDIAN

It's kind of you to consider me.

PRODUCER

You're precisely what I want. A natural, a natural.

COMEDIAN

What do you mean, a natural? I work hard,
arrive at my effects by trial and error,
by calculating rigidly. Now take
my entrance in the second jungle scene for instance . . .

MANAGER

This new part is a dream, a scream, a jewel of
a part, a hell of a wonderful opportunity. What's
more you'll earn more money than you ever
dreamed of. The Fabulous Producer means to
feature you; get that? To *feature* you. Your
name in lights maybe.

PRODUCER

And it will be the first time that an actor of
your race has been so honored. Think of it:
featured in the Fabulous Producer's new revue,
your name in lights. I have it—your name
spelled out in red lights, red.

COMEDIAN

What is my role to be?

MANAGER

Tremendous, superb. You'll see.

PRODUCER

All your effortless talents, all your natural gifts . . .

COMEDIAN

I work hard, there's nothing so effortless . . .

MANAGER & PRODUCER

We know, we know.

PRODUCER

All your natural gifts will have full play. Now in
the big jungle scene . . .

COMEDIAN

Jungle scene? Jungle scene?

MANAGER

A riotous scene, a colorful scene, a scintillant scene.

COMEDIAN

But what is different, what is new about. . . ?

PRODUCER

You are a zulu king in leopard skin, stiff Cady.

COMEDIAN

You can't be serious. That isn't new. You saw
me play that role tonight.

MANAGER

You'll be made. You'll be the town's delight.

PRODUCER

You sit on a throne made of two luminous dice and drink a
bottle of rum. You do a dance.

MANAGER

Boy, they'll go crazy when you dance. And when you come
out in the purple suit in the big plantation scene. . . .

COMEDIAN

Gentlemen, goodnight. I am not in the least interested.
You're only wasting time.

PRODUCER

You see a Bengal tiger in the moonlight and you run away.

MANAGER

Excruciating, captivating. You wear a pair of big white spats.

PRODUCER

I brought the contract with me. Please sign here.

MANAGER

And here's a pen.

COMEDIAN

I do not want the part. I will not sign.

PRODUCER

What?

MANAGER

You lost your mind, boy? No one turns down a
contract offered by the Fabulous Producer.

PRODUCER

And remember, I'm prepared to feature you. The
first time one of your race has been so honored.

COMEDIAN

Honor, indeed! I'm tired of clowning. If I
am to play a king, why not let me play
a king, and not a hackneyed parody of one?
I do not want the part, so goodnight, gentlemen.

MANAGER

Not so fast, boy, not so fast.

PRODUCER

The part was made for you. There's no one else I'd . . .

COMEDIAN

Isn't it true that you intend to offer
Richard the Second next season?

PRODUCER

Yes, I do. But I hardly see what that has to do
with our discussion here.

COMEDIAN

Just this: I know the role. I have rehearsed
those lines a thousand times. Give me the chance
to play King Richard.

PRODUCER

Well, I, . . . that is . . . you understand . . .

MANAGER

We'd all lose money. People want to laugh. They wouldn't
take you serious. You're a . . . a . . . comedian anyway.

PRODUCER

That's it. You're a . . . a . . . comedian. They wouldn't want
a . . .

COMEDIAN

A black king, you mean. And you don't either.
Please go. There's no more to say.

MANAGER

You better think it over. This show will close, then where will
you be? And you're in debt to me, remember. All those fried
chicken dinners for your high-yaller lady friends. You better
think it over. (*He takes contract from Producer, lays it on Comedian's dressing table.*)

*He exits with the Producer. The Comedian picks up contract and
starts to tear it in two, but stops, reflects, lays it down. The light in the
tall mirror appears again: the marionette, dressed now like a musical
comedy African, cavorts about the puppet stage.*

*The Comedian toys with the contract. He leans against the dressing
table in deeply troubled thought as the Puppet dances whirlingly. In a
little while the light in the mirror goes out, followed by the lights at the
dressing table. For a moment the stage is in complete darkness.*

*The light comes on again inside the mirror, which has become a
sort of portrait-frame stage hung with silver curtains. Three Masked
Figures enter and seat themselves before the stage. The silver curtains
part, revealing a dimly lighted scene, a richly figured arras, a carved
throne.*

*The Comedian is seated upon the throne. He wears a crown and a
voluminous robe, and he holds a sceptre in his hand, reminiscent of
the cane carried earlier in that it, too, is tied with brightly colored*

ribbons. In a moment, the Comedian rises with great dignity. Offstage a scratched and indistinct phonograph recording of a man's voice giving a dramatic recitation is played. And the Comedian's gestures follow the rhythms of the monolog.

The Three Masked Figures watch the Comedian-King's stylized gestures with great interest.

After a while the recording seems not to end but simply to slow down to a stop, as though the phonograph needed winding. The silver curtains close. Then there are loud applause offstage and cries of "Bravo!" The curtains open, and the player comes forward to take his bow.

The Three Masked Figures stand. Each has a large flower in his hand and advances with a kind of stylized dance movement to present it to the Comedian. As the last one bestows his tribute, a low chanting of "Black . . . Black . . . Black" begins off stage. The three figures point to the Comedian and confer among themselves. The applause changes to hisses and catcalls.

The Three Masked Figures turn and come downstage, jerking their heads in direction of stage where the Comedian stands now transfixed with horror. The masks they wear can be clearly seen at this point—distorted, hideous with cruelty and bigotry. In time to the chanting of "Black . . . Black . . ." they hitch and jiggle, trying to decide what to do. At last they rush to the mirror-stage, and one of them snatches off the Comedian's robe, revealing the sunflower coat beneath. They point and laugh in pantomime, misshapen heads lolling and twisting.

The Comedian cringes and falls back. Offstage the chanting of "Black" has given way to loud slaughtering laughter which reaches a crescendo of mockery as the lights go out.

When the lights come on again, the Comedian is at the dressing-table as before. He shakes off his dreadful revery. He picks up the contract again, looks toward the large mirror with a shudder. Then he puts on his coat, takes out a pen and signs the paper.

The Puppet appears, apes the Comedian's motions as he signs his name. The Comedian puts the contract into his pocket, puts on his hat. He turns out the dressing table light and leaves. The Puppet is furiously whirling and leaping and grimacing as the curtain falls.

II

Essays and Introductions

Counterpoise

we are unalterably opposed to the chauvinistic, the cultish, to
special pleading, to all that seeks to limit and restrict creative
expression

we believe experimentation to be an absolute necessity in
keeping the arts vital and significant in contemporary life;
therefore we support and encourage the experimental and
the unconventional in writing, music and the graphic arts,
though we do not consider our own work avant-garde in the
accepted sense of the term

as writers who belong to a so-called minority we are violently
opposed to having our work viewed, as the custom is, entirely
in the light of sociology and politics

to having it overpraised on the one hand by those with an axe
to grind or with a conscience to salve

to having it misinterpreted on the other hand by coterie edi-
tors, reviewers, anthologists who refuse us encouragement or

This manifesto was written in about 1948 for an introductory leaflet
to the Counterpoise Series (Nashville: Hemphill Press, ca. 1948).
For this series Hayden edited four booklets of poetry and fiction.

critical guidance because we deal with realities we find it neither possible nor desirable to ignore

as poets we naturally believe that it is more profitable for our generation to read good poetry than it is to listen to soap opera, since poetry has humanistic and spiritual values not to be ignored with impunity

we believe in the oneness of mankind and the importance of the arts in the struggle for peace and unity

Twentieth-Century American Poetry

Much that has occurred in contemporary American poetry can be seen as the culmination of tendencies originating in the nineteenth century with Walt Whitman, Emily Dickinson, and, to some extent, Stephen Crane. These poets are now generally considered to have been innovators, forerunners of modernism. And during the 1920s literary rebels eagerly claimed them as spiritual ancestors whose work had helped prepare the way for the New Poetry movement.

Known also as the Poetry Revival, the New Poetry movement began in London as an international phenomenon before the First World War. Ezra Pound, the brilliant expatriate American poet, encouraged poets to break with the past in order to achieve greater freedom of expression. Pound's theories led to the concept of Imagism, which owed something to French Symbolism as well as to oriental and ancient Greek poetry. In the group of young poets attracted to the ideals of Imagism were the Americans John Gould Fletcher, Amy Lowell, Hilda Doolittle (who became well known as H.D.), and her English husband, Richard Aldington.

From *The United States in Literature,* edited by James E. Miller, Jr., Robert Hayden, and Robert O'Neal. Copyright © 1973 by Scott, Foresman and Company. Reprinted by permission. Hayden assisted with the editing of this textbook and of several others for Scott, Foresman.

The Imagists (they sometimes referred to themselves rather artily as *Les Imagistes*) received attention for several years as a distinct group and had some influence on Carl Sandburg, Wallace Stevens, and Marianne Moore. Ezra Pound was their acknowledged leader, editing *Des Imagistes* in 1914 and publishing essays and manifestoes. He defined the principles of imagism as precision of diction and image, freedom in the choice of subjects, and a controlled freedom of rhythm based on musical cadence and not on traditional meters—free verse, in other words, which gave to the New Poetry movement the alternate name of the Free Verse Revolt.

The revolt against poetic conventions had started early in the twentieth century. Two great poets, Edwin Arlington Robinson and Robert Frost, had already produced fresh and original work by the end of the first decade. Ignored at first, they later emerged as luminaries of the Poetry Revival. But in 1912, Harriet Monroe published the first number of *Poetry: A Magazine of Verse* in Chicago. This magazine was of strategic importance, providing a medium for the work of poets here and abroad, disseminating the new poetic theories, and bringing them into focus and to the attention of the public.

The New Poetry movement, somewhat tentative during the war years, gained momentum in the 1920s. Now popularly referred to as the "Jazz Age," this was a period of drastic social change, a time of experimentation in lifestyles as well as in the arts. The "modern mode" in literature was firmly established during the decade. Changes in moral outlook transformed poetic vision and technique. Poets sought to free their art from the gentility and didacticism of the previous generation. Freudian psychology, the changing status of women, the development of science and technology—all suggested new possibilities for poetry. Religious skepticism, growing since the last century, and the moral disillusionment caused by the war were recurrent themes in the new poetry.

American poets were frequently critics of society. Edna St. Vincent Millay, for example, in "Justice Denied in Massachusetts" protested what she and many of her contemporaries believed to be a miscarriage of justice in the execution of the philosophical anarchists, Sacco and Vanzetti. James Weldon Johnson, Claude McKay, and Countee Cullen spoke out in eloquent, often passionate, lyrics against racial injustice. Sandburg, Robinson, and Vachel Lindsay, among others, expressed their distrust of American materialism. The spiritual emptiness of an industrialized civilization, the sense of alienation and futility experienced by many individuals in the modern world were the central themes of T. S. Eliot's "The Love Song of J. Alfred Prufrock" and *The Waste Land.*

But if poets were critics of twentieth-century life, they were also explorers engaged in exciting voyages of discovery. They turned to the American past for subjects and made use of indigenous folk materials. Some looked for a genuine "American rhythm," seeking it in jazz and spirituals, in the poetry and song of the American Indian. Folk heroes and legendary figures were celebrated in ballads and other forms of narrative poetry—Abe Lincoln, John Brown, Paul Bunyan, John Henry, Johnny Appleseed, etc. Poems derived from history and myth quite often blended psychological realism with romantic elements. A notable example was *John Brown's Body* (1926), Stephen Vincent Benét's book-length poem about the Civil War. Robinson, Frost, Sandburg, Edgar Lee Masters, and Lindsay, whose careers had started before the twenties, continued to write what may be called "poetry in the American grain."

It was Vachel Lindsay who helped the Afro-American poet Langston Hughes gain early recognition. Hughes was a busboy at the Washington hotel where Lindsay stayed during one of his "vaudeville" tours, and Hughes ventured to show the famous poet a few of his poems. Lindsay was so enthusiastic that he included some of them in a public reading and afterwards told newspaper reporters about his discovery of a talented young black poet. Hughes subsequently became a leading figure in the Harlem Renaissance and, eventually, one of America's best-known poets.

The Harlem Renaissance, known also as the New Negro movement and the Negro Renaissance, was an important cultural manifestation of the mid-twenties. With Harlem as its center, the Renaissance was an upsurge of new racial attitudes and ideals on the part of Afro-Americans and an artistic and political awakening. It was partly inspired by the iconoclastic spirit of the times. The Harlem writers and artists were, like their white counterparts, in quest of new images, forms, techniques. They too were skeptical and disillusioned. What chiefly differentiated them, however, was their view of artistic endeavor as an extension of the struggle against oppression.

Besides Langston Hughes, the poets who achieved recognition during the Renaissance were Claude McKay, Countee Cullen (whose first book *Color* [1925] was published while he was still in college), Jean Toomer, and Arna Bontemps. James Weldon Johnson was a distinguished older poet associated with the New Negro movement and, together with its chief spokesman, Alain Locke, was honored as a mentor. Writing in both free and conventional verse, the Harlem poets expressed racial bitterness and racial pride more boldly than their predecessors had ever done. They affirmed their African heritage in poems often filled with exotic imagery, celebrating the "primitive" forces pulsing under the black man's veneer of civilization. This tendency to emphasize the primitive and exotic provoked the charge that the New Negroes replaced old stereotypes with new ones equally objectionable. Countee Cullen's "Heritage," which appeared in his second volume, *Copper Sun* (1927) was one of the best of these atavistic poems, although the Africa it describes is literary and romanticized.

Jazz rhythms, images from big-city life (Harlem's in particular), and themes from history and folklore were found in the works of the Renaissance poets, several of whom were also novelists. Claude McKay's *Home to Harlem* (1928) contained poems that expressed something of the bittersweet quality of life in that city within a city. Jean Toomer's *Cane* (1923) was a volume of poems, sketches, and stories garnered from his experiences in the South and from his impressions of Afro-American life in the North. Blues and jazz suggested motifs and verse patterns for Langston Hughes's first book, *The Weary*

Blues (1926). Arna Bontemps, who did not publish a book of his poetry during the Renaissance, contributed reflective personal lyrics and poems evoking a sense of the Negro past to *The Crisis* and *Opportunity*, magazines that encouraged the Harlem writers by publishing their writing and awarding various prizes.

The New Negro movement had some effect upon writers outside of the Harlem group, stimulating interest in Afro-American life and problems. Carl Van Vechten and Eugene O'Neill were among those who used material from this source. The movement had run its course by 1930.

By the 1930s the ideals of the New Poetry had been accepted and no longer seemed radical or even controversial. Free verse was the preferred technique of many poets, and although Imagism as a distinct movement no longer existed, it was still a minor influence. Significant work in traditional forms continued, of course. Robinson published philosophical lyrics and narrative poems written in flexible yet definite metrical patterns. Robert Frost pursued what he called his "lover's quarrel with the world" in verse forms that were conventional, though the poet's vision and tone were highly individual. Personal and metaphysical poetry employing meter and rhyme often achieved notable distinction through the artistry of Edna St. Vincent Millay, Countee Cullen, Paul Engle, and Elinor Wylie.

The twentieth century is often described as an era of rapid, almost breathless change. Fashions in the arts change not by the generation but by the decade, though, inevitably, much is carried over from one period to the next, as a constant among the variables. Yet each decade has its own imprimatur, its own special focus. During the thirties, social consciousness and political awareness gave special impetus to American poetry.

Marxist radicalism, the labor struggle, the Depression, and the menace of Fascism determined the form and content of much of the literature of the period. Left-wing critics defined the role of the poet as that of propagandist, spokesman for a cause: the poet was to be a voice for the inarticulate masses, championing the oppressed victims of an unjust social order.

The poetry written from this point of view was usually of negligible literary value, not because of its content primarily, but because it was more rhetorical and programmatic than imaginative. The question of whether a valid distinction between art and propaganda could really be made was hotly debated in these years, and remains a controversial question today.

A great deal of socially conscious verse has lost its patina, retaining only a certain period interest, if any. There are, however, some exceptions. Much of the poetry of Archibald MacLeish and Kenneth Fearing was written out of a deep concern over injustice and human exploitation, and has not entirely lost its vitality and relevance. Langston Hughes, Margaret Walker, Frank Marshall Davis, and Richard Wright wrote perceptively about the Afro-American condition.

Carl Sandburg's *The People, Yes* (1936) was evidence of the continuing interest in the folk culture shared by a number of artists during the period. The songs, oral literature, and customs of unsophisticated people not only suggested themes for poems, but were also regarded as indications of basic strengths and virtues necessary for fundamental social change.

Undoubtedly, the best political poetry of the thirties was written by W. H. Auden, the English poet who eventually became an American citizen. Auden revealed his left-wing sympathies in poems that were technically brilliant and intellectually complex reflections on the dilemmas of modern society. Auden was wry, mocking, satiric. His command of technique, the range of his diction and imagery, his ability to use every poetic device available marked him from the outset as a major poet. Other poets learned from him, and he attracted followers who imitated his style. By the end of the thirties, Auden had turned away from Marxism, having come to regard it as a threat to individual freedom.

Like Auden, other poets also underwent a change of heart, caught up in the moral crises brought on by the Second World War. The bitter moral implications of war gave focus and intensity to the poetry of Marianne Moore, Gwendolyn

Brooks, Karl Shapiro, Randall Jarrell, and Richard Eberhart. None of these poets harbored any romantic illusions about the glories of war. Together with other poets of the period they gave their readers, in precise and unsentimental language and striking imagery, an idea of the enormities of global conflict and the human suffering and debasement it caused.

During the war years and after, poetry tended to grow more subjective and metaphysical. Since many poets made use of private references closed to the general reader, poetry also became more obscure, and was often criticized as being too "intellectual," and sometimes derided as poetry written only for professional critics. Of course, some poets did try to conform to the principles of the New Criticism formulated by John Crowe Ransom, Allen Tate, Cleanth Brooks, and Robert Penn Warren, all of whom (with the exception of Brooks) were well-known Southern poets. The New Critics emphasized the importance of formal structure, were partial to metaphysical verse, and frowned on social statement as inimical to the spirit of poetry.

Nevertheless, the poetry of T. S. Eliot, Robert Lowell, and W. H. Auden reflected the spiritual crisis of the forties. Tightly packed and often strenuously intellectual, their poetry involved complicated metrical and stanzaic patterns, and formed part of the revival of interest in form. In general the influence of the New Criticism produced poetry of elegant phrasing, carefully wrought images and textures, and a respect for meticulous craftsmanship which characterized the earlier work of Richard Wilbur, Karl Shapiro, Randall Jarrell, John Ciardi, and Gwendolyn Brooks. Theodore Roethke was, in a sense, "wilder" than any of these poets, cultivating the irrational and surrealistic in free-form lyrics, voicing the terrors and beauties of existence and the natural world of growing things. Yet he was an accomplished writer of strictly patterned poems as well.

In the 1950s a negative reaction to formalism became apparent. The theories of the New Critics were challenged as irrelevant. The supremacy of Auden and Eliot was challenged by poets who took as their guides Ezra Pound and William Carlos Williams. Ezra Pound's poetry seemed to a new generation of poets the greatest work of the century. Pound's admirers were loud in their praise of him as the "originator" of modern poetry, but not everyone was prepared to go that far or to ignore the fact that Pound sometimes used his poetry as a vehicle for reactionary ideas. Although a controversial figure, Pound has been—as critic, poet, translator, polemicist—one of the major influences on twentieth-century literature. William Carlos Williams, physician and poet, was Pound's friend during his lifetime but did not share his views. Influenced in the early years of his career by Imagism, Williams subsequently wrote free-verse lyrics in what he thought of as an "American rhythm." Avoiding meter, he took the cadences of native speech as the basis for his rhythms. Everyday experiences, familiar objects, seemingly trivial actions or events, fleeting moments of recognition or awareness are among the typical materials he developed into poems with precision and, for the most part, without moralizing.

Williams and Pound, together with Walt Whitman, of course, were lauded by the emergent "Beat" poets of the mid-1950s as the natural enemies of formalist theory and practice. However, in their eagerness to rid poetry of artiness and elitism many Beat poets emphasized "communication" and "self-expression" at the expense of craftsmanship, and wrote poems which were banal, imprecise, and pretentious. With the Beat poets, figurative language fell into disfavor, and came to be regarded as a literary "cop-out," an evasion of reality.

The Beat phenomenon, centered for a while in New York's Greenwich Village and the North Beach area of San Francisco, signified a withdrawal from society by those who were contemptuous of its materialism and conformity. To be "beat" was to be tired of, worn out by, a corrupt world. It also connoted the rebelling individual's quest for "beatitude"—a beatific state induced by voluntary privation, anarchistic individualism, rock music, esoteric religious cults, drugs, sex.

Allen Ginsberg's *Howl* (1956), the central poem of the Beat movement, cries out against the destruction of "the best minds of my generation," yet concludes with the affirmation that life, however sordid and vicious, is holy. Among other Beats who earned popular recognition was Lawrence Ferlinghetti, writer of poems that blend fantasy, wit, and whimsy into an oblique commentary on the condition of modern man. Beat poetry waned in the sixties, and many of its energies poured into the mainstream of American poetry. Robert Creeley and Denise Levertov, for example, absorbed the Beat vitality and won reputations as influential avant-garde poets writing in the traditions of Pound and Williams.

American poetry at the present time exhibits great creative energy and a variety of styles and themes. As in the earlier decades of the century, poets continue to experiment with form and language, and poetry has become increasingly free in structure, increasingly "realistic" in subject matter. "Open" forms of "free" verse—that is, poetry without definite metrical pattern—is a characteristic mode of the period, although it is not the only one. Many outstanding poets still use meter and rhyme, but they, like their experimental contemporaries, are more influenced by the rhythms and textures of natural speech than by the old prosodic requirements. The prevalent feeling among most poets today is that all areas of human experience are appropriate for poetry. Hence, materials that in the past were considered at best too mundane for poetry and at worst offensive and improper are now freely used.

In preceding centuries critics and poets themselves were often concerned with the problem of an appropriate vocabulary for poetry—poetic diction. Slang and coarse expressions, common in recent poetry, were not approved by the arbiters of literary taste, although such major British poets as Shakespeare and William Blake frequently went beyond the limits of elegance and refinement. William Wordsworth, in nineteenth-century England, held that poetry should be written in the language of "common men." The Scottish poet Robert Burns used dialect and folk expressions in his poems about Scottish life. Gerard Manley Hopkins (in late nineteenth-century England) frequently employed terms from the workaday world as well as outmoded and even made-up words.

Walt Whitman was undoubtedly the most daring of these early innovators. His *Leaves of Grass* offended many readers who considered his diction rough and "barbaric" and his references to the body, to sex, indelicate. In his efforts to encompass everything he did not hesitate to make use of slang and the vernacular—the language of "common men." And he was a pioneer in the use of free verse, rejecting conventional meters and stanza patterns in favor of a more flexible and individual kind of poetry.

Twentieth-century poets have gone much further in regard to diction and subject matter than Whitman. In order to get away from the "literary," poets like Allen Ginsberg and LeRoi Jones have employed slang and "four-letter" words, and they have sometimes consciously resorted to triteness and banality in order to bring their poems closer to everyday life and speech. The results are not always admirable or even interesting. Modern poets feel free to use any word that contributes to the expression of a theme or idea. The concept of a special vocabulary for poetry—"poetic diction"—has long since been abandoned.

Much of the poetry published in our country in recent years can be classified as the poetry of social awareness. It is poetry with a purpose and registers the social and moral pressures of our times. The Vietnam War, racial strife, such national tragedies as the assassinations of John and Robert Kennedy and Martin Luther King—all these have inspired poetic response.

The emergence of a so-called school of Black Poetry in America has been one of the significant literary developments of the modern period. Although the Harlem Renaissance of the 1920s brought certain Afro-American poets into prominence, it was not until the intensification of the civil rights struggle during the 1960s that a separate group of black poets began to take shape. Avowedly nationalistic (that is, racially proud) and scornful of Western aesthetics, these poets continued the protest tradition, historically associated with Negro writers. But they were more radical in outlook than their predecessors. Unlike the Harlem group, they rejected entry into the mainstream of American literature as a desirable goal. They insisted that their poetry could not be judged by white standards, urging its importance as an expression of black consciousness.

LeRoi Jones—the most influential of the young activist poets—Don L. Lee, Nikki Giovanni, Sonia Sanchez, Mari Evans, Etheridge Knight, and David Henderson all attune their lyres to the "black aesthetic." Not yet satisfactorily defined, this term, originating in the sixties, may be interpreted as a sense of the spiritual and artistic values of blackness. It is, perhaps, a logical (some would say "chauvinistic") reaction to negative American racial attitudes. Perhaps the concept is best summarized by the slogan "Black is beautiful." Those who accept this point of view regard Negro subject matter as their exclusive domain, feeling that only those who have shared "black experience" can articulate it. Older poets whose work shows some alignment with the new Black Poetry include Margaret Walker and Gwendolyn Brooks, winner of the Pulitzer Prize in 1950.

Whether poetry should be valued primarily for the unique inner experience it can provide or for its effectiveness as political or social statement is a question that often recurs in discussions of the true functions of the art today.

It has been impossible, of course, to do more than sketch in the main lines of poetic development. But even from so brief an account as this we can gain, perhaps, some idea of the directions our poetry has taken. Changes in attitude toward the function of poetry, experimentation, the use of materials once thought unpoetic have largely determined its course. Yet the formal and traditional have never been completely discarded, though they have been modified by the tastes and the preoccupations of the age.

American poets have frequently been criticized for their negative view of life in general and of American society in particular. It is true that many of them have given voice to doubt and pessimism. Yet the act of creation itself is an act of faith, a kind of affirmation, and the poetry of disillusionment often implies a moral concern with things as they ought to be, a vision of something better than we have.

The present century is a time of expanding consciousness, a time when new frontiers are being opened and new possibilities of life and art investigated. The concepts of God and the universe, of man and society, are in process of revision. Poetry can offer us no solutions to our dilemmas, nor is it intended to, but it can help us understand ourselves at this stage of human evolution. It can make us aware. And it can give us a special kind of joy.

Introduction to *Kaleidoscope:*
Poems by American Negro Poets

The question whether we can speak with any real justification of "Negro poetry" arises often today. Some object to the term because it has been used disparagingly to indicate a kind of pseudo-poetry concerned with the race problem to the exclusion of almost everything else. Others hold that Negro poetry per se could only be produced in black Africa. Seen from this point of view, the poetry of the American Negro, its "specialized" content notwithstanding, is obviously not to be thought of as existing apart from the rest of our literature, but as having been shaped over some three centuries by social, moral, and literary forces essentially American.

Those who presently avow themselves "poets of the Negro revolution" argue that they do indeed constitute a separate group or school, since the purpose of their writing is to give Negroes a sense of human dignity and provide them with ideological weapons. A belligerent race pride moves these celebrants of Black Power to declare themselves not simply "poets," but "Negro poets." However, Countee Cullen, the brilliant lyricist of the Harlem Renaissance in the 1920s, insisted that he be considered a "poet," not a "Negro poet," for he did not want to be restricted to racial themes nor have his poetry judged solely on the basis of its relevance to the Negro struggle.

Cullen was aware of a peculiar risk Negro poets have had to face. The tendency of American critics has been to label the established Negro writer a "spokesman for his race." There are, as we have seen, poets who think of themselves in that role. But the effect of such labeling is to place any Negro author in a kind of literary ghetto where the standards applied to other writers are not likely to be applied to him, since he, being a "spokesman for his race," is not considered primarily a writer but a species of race-relations man, the leader of a cause, the voice of protest.

Protest has been a recurring element in the writing of American Negroes, a fact hardly to be wondered at, given the social conditions under which they have been forced to live. And the Negro poet's devotion to the cause of freedom is not in any way reprehensible, for throughout history poets have often been champions of human liberty. But bad poetry is another matter, and there is no denying that a great deal of "race poetry" is poor, because its content seems ready-made and art is displaced by argument.

Phillis Wheatley (ca. 1750–1784), the first poet of African descent to win some measure of recognition, had almost nothing to say about the plight of her people. And if she resented her own ambiguous position in society, she did not express her resentment. One reason for her silence is that, although brought to Boston as a slave, she never lived as one. Another is that as a neoclassical poet she would scarcely have thought it proper to reveal much of herself in her poetry, although we do get brief glimpses of her in the poem addressed to the Earl of Dartmouth and in "On Being Brought from Africa to America." Neoclassicism emphasized reason rather than emotion and favored elegance and formality. The English poet, Alexander Pope, was the acknowledged master of this style, and in submitting to his influence Phillis Wheatley produced poetry that was as good as that of her American contemporaries. She actually wrote better than some of them.

But the poetry of Phillis Wheatley and her fellow poet,

Jupiter Hammon, has historical and not literary interest for us now. The same can be said of much of eighteenth-century American poetry in general. Not until the nineteenth century did the United States begin to have literature of unqualified merit and originality. There were no Negro poets of stature in the period before the Civil War, but there were several with talent, among them George Moses Horton (1797–ca.1883) and Frances E. W. Harper (1825–1911). Didactic and sentimental, they wrote with competence and moral fervor in the manner of their times. Their poetry is remembered chiefly because it contributed to the antislavery struggle, and because it testifies to the creative efforts of Negroes under disheartening conditions.

During the Reconstruction era, writers of "local color" turned for material to the history, the customs, and the dialect that made each section of the country different from the others. James Whitcomb Riley published poems in the Hoosier dialect of Indiana. White Southern authors wrote nostalgically of the Old South and through their idealization of antebellum plantation life created the "plantation tradition" in literature. Thomas Nelson Page, for example, wrote Negro dialect verse that was an apology for slavery, picturing the Negro as docile and happy in servitude. Both Riley and Page had some influence on Paul Laurence Dunbar (1872–1906), the most important Negro poet to emerge in the latter part of the century.

Some of Dunbar's dialect verse is in the plantation tradition, but it is essentially different from the kind written by the Southern apologists, his portrayals of Negro life being more sympathetic and more authentic. Dunbar became famous for his work in this medium, and other Negro poets imitated him. But he himself put less value on his dialect verse than he did on his poems in standard English.

In the twentieth century Negro poets have abandoned dialect for an idiom truer to folk speech. The change has been due not only to differences in social outlook on their part but also to revolutionary developments in American poetry. The New Poetry movement, which began before the First World

War and reached its definitive point in the 1920s, represented a break with the past. Free verse, diction close to everyday speech, a realistic approach to life, and the use of material once considered unpoetic—these were the goals of the movement. The Negro poet-critic, William Stanley Braithwaite, encouraged the "new" poetry through his articles in the *Boston Evening Transcript* and his yearly anthologies of magazine verse.

The New Negro movement or Negro Renaissance, resulting from the social, political, and artistic awakening of Negroes in the twenties, brought into prominence poets whose work showed the influence of the poetic revolution. Protest became more defiant, racial bitterness and racial pride more outspoken than ever before. Negro history and folklore were explored as new sources of inspiration. Spirituals, blues, and jazz suggested themes and verse patterns to young poets like Jean Toomer and Langston Hughes. Certain conventions, notably what has been called "literary Garveyism," grew out of a fervent Negro nationalism. Marcus Garvey, leader of the United Negro Improvement Association, advocated a "return" to Africa, the lost homeland, and nearly all the Renaissance poets wrote poems about their spiritual ties to Africa, about the dormant fires of African paganism in the Negro soul that the white man's civilization could never extinguish. Countee Cullen's "Heritage" is one of the best of these poems, even though the Africa it presents is artificial, romanticized, and it reiterates exotic clichés in vogue during the period when it was written.

Harlem was the center of the Negro Renaissance, which for that reason is also referred to as the Harlem Renaissance. Two magazines, *The Crisis* and *Opportunity*, gave aid and encouragement to Negro writers by publishing their work and by awarding literary prizes.

In the decades since the New Negro movement, which ended with the twenties, protest and race consciousness have continued to find expression in the poetry of the American Negro. But other motivating forces are also in evidence. There are Negro poets who believe that any poet's most clearly defined task is to create with honesty and sincerity poems that will illuminate human experience—not exclusively "Negro experience." They reject the idea of poetry as racial propaganda, of poetry that functions as a kind of sociology. Their attitude is not wholly new, of course, being substantially that of Dunbar and Cullen. In counterpoise to it is the "Beat" or "nonacademic" view held by poets who are not only in rebellion against middle-class ideals and the older poetic traditions but who also advocate a militant racism in a definitely "Negro" poetry.

It has come to be expected of Negro poets that they will address themselves to the race question—and that they will all say nearly the same things about it. Such "group unity" is more apparent than real. Differences in vision and emphasis, fundamental differences in approach to the art of poetry itself, modify and give diversity to the writing of these poets, even when they employ similar themes. And certainly there is no agreement among them as to what the much-debated role of the Negro poet should be.

This anthology is not intended as a comprehensive survey, but, rather, as a guide that will help students gain some notion of the salient features of a particular area of the American literary landscape. Not all the selections will be read with the same degree of interest, but it is hoped that the majority of them will afford enjoyment and deepen the appreciation of poetry.

Perhaps it would not be amiss to say in conclusion that neither the editor nor his publisher should be understood as necessarily endorsing the long-established custom of segregating the work of Negro poets within the covers of a separate anthology. Yet where, except in a collection such as the present one, is the student to gather any impression of the nature and scope of the Negro's contribution to American poetry?

Preface to *The New Negro*

Dr. Alain Locke's interpretive anthology, *The New Negro,* first published in 1925, was the definitive presentation of the artistic and social goals of the New Negro movement. Perhaps it is no exaggeration to say that this book helped to create the movement. Certainly it had the effect of a manifesto when it appeared, and it remains an invaluable document of the cultural aspects of the Negro struggle as they were revealed by the work of artists and writers in Harlem during the 1920s.

The New Negro movement, known also as the Harlem Renaissance and the Negro Renaissance, was less a movement, as we generally use the term, than a configuration of "new" racial attitudes and ideals and the upsurge of creativity inspired by them and by the iconoclastic spirit of the times. In his introductory essay to *The New Negro* Dr. Locke described the movement as representing a new spiritual outlook, as having "inner objectives." And he saw the Negro's "newness" as the product of psychic and social forces that had been gathering strength since the nineteenth century.

The New Negro movement had no formal organization, and it was more aesthetic and philosophical—more metaphysical, let us say—than political. Such political implications as it now may be seen to have had arose from the fervid

Negro nationalism which was its background and which became significant after the First World War. One of the most zealous voices of black nationalism was Marcus Garvey, West Indian leader of the United Negro Improvement Association. He is mentioned only briefly, and somewhat disparagingly, in the pages of *The New Negro*. Yet Garveyism had tremendous appeal for American Negroes, winning thousands of ardent followers who saw in its program of separatism and its vision of a mass "return" to Africa their best hope for liberation and autonomy.

Africa was a recurrent theme of the Harlem writers, whose atavistic poems and stories later came to be classified, more or less humorously, as "literary Garveyism." African art as a vital source of inspiration for the Negro artist was discussed by Dr. Locke in "The Legacy of the Ancestral Arts." And although he considered Garveyism a "transient, if spectacular phenomenon," he believed nonetheless that "the possible role of the American Negro in the future development of Africa is one of the most constructive and universally helpful missions that any modern people can lay claim to."

The Negro Renaissance was of short duration, beginning in the mid-twenties and ending with the decade. Harlem was its acknowledged center. A Negro city within a city, bohemian, cosmopolitan, "fast"; vibrant locus of a variety of racial strains, nationalities, languages, dialects, folkways; a "city of refuge" where "group expression and self-determination" would be possible—Harlem attracted young Negro artists and intellectuals from all over the United States and from foreign countries as well. They came, together with hosts of less articulate migrants fleeing Southern oppression, to seek fulfillment in the Negro "Culture Capital," as Harlem was designated by the Renaissance group.

Too often the Harlem Renaissance, when given any attention at all in the textbooks, is approached as though it had no organic relationship to the developments taking place in American culture generally during the twenties. That the converse was true is amply illustrated by this anthology.

"The Jazz Age" was a period of disillusionment and revolt,

of experimentation in lifestyles and in the various forms of imaginative expression. The accent was on the "new" and untried. Old modes were either rejected or were revaluated and adapted to the uses of an often self-conscious modernism. Americans, black and white, sought to discover or to reclaim their native spiritual resources. Mary Austin looked for the authentic "American rhythm" in Indian poetry and song. The Negro became a "vogue," partly as the result of a growing interest in his jazz, spirituals, and folklore, partly as the result of the glamour and notoriety brought to the Harlem Renaissance by wealthy dilettantes who "took it up" as a sort of amusing hobby.

The Negro Renaissance was clearly an expression of the Zeitgeist, and its writers and artists were open to the same influences that their white counterparts were. What differentiated the New Negroes from other American intellectuals was their race consciousness, their group awareness, their sense of sharing a common purpose. Arna Bontemps, poet, and novelist, has said in the foreword to his book of poems, *Personals* (London, 1963):

> It did not take long to discover that I was just one of many young Negroes arriving in Harlem for the first time and with many of the same thoughts and intentions. Within a year or two we began to recognize ourselves as a "group" and to become a little self-conscious about our "significance." When we were not too busy having fun, we were shown off and exhibited and presented in scores of places to all kinds of people. And we heard the sighs of wonder, amazement and sometimes admiration when it was whispered or announced that here was one of the "New Negroes."

But if it arouses nostalgia in those who once shared in its novelty and excitement, the movement also elicits the animadversions of a later generation that feels it was essentially bourgeois, genteel, and lacking in political dynamism. Some critics have charged that the New Negroes "went in" for a fashionable exoticism, cultivating a species of primitivism in the arts which was calculated to appeal to a jaded white audience. The Harlem writers, it is often said, simply exchanged one set of racial clichés for another. And, further, their identification with Africa was a mere pose, a literary convention.

In March 1925, Dr. Alain Locke, then Professor of Philosophy at Howard University and one of the chief mentors of the Renaissance, edited the Harlem number of the *Survey Graphic*. The materials originally gathered for the magazine became the nucleus for *The New Negro*. Dr. Locke's stated purpose was to "register the transformations of the inner and outer life of the Negro in America that [had] so significantly taken place in the last few years."

Including sociological and historical essays, poetry, fiction, drama, and criticism, this handsomely designed book covered every phase of recent Negro cultural achievement. There had been nothing like it before. Sophisticated and urbane, race conscious without being chauvinistic—there were several white contributors, for instance—it presented facets of Negro life and thought which stimulated the imagination and challenged traditional prejudices. One of its most exciting and unusual features was the work of the Austrian artist Winold Reiss and the rising young Negro artist Aaron Douglas. Their illustrations, portraits of racial types and African-inspired decorative motifs, constituted a fresh and original approach to materials hitherto little explored. Together with the photographs of African sculpture also included, the work of these artists added considerably to the total effect of the volume as a testimonial to Negro beauty, dignity, and creativity. Stressing the role of the Negro writer as the interpreter of his people, Dr. Locke drew upon the work of Countee Cullen, Jean Toomer, Langston Hughes, and Claude McKay, all of whom had won recognition. Older writers whose work was considered to have prepared the way for the Harlem avant-garde were represented by James Weldon Johnson and W. E. B. DuBois, among others.

The cachet of the modern mode, still in the process of becoming during this period, reveals itself in *The New Negro* with varying degrees of luster. Realism and satire are characteristic styles, as are symbolism and impressionism. Disenchantment and skepticism are present too. An interest in the experimental and a concern with new forms and techniques are much in evidence. Certain poems and stories, notably those of Jean Toomer and Eric Walrond, have an exotic flavor, a tropical lushness. Others achieve distinctive rhythms and individuality of tone and idiom through the use of Negro folk motifs.

The New Negro writers rejected the "minstrel tradition" in American literature, with its caricatures and Southern dialect, and they likewise rejected overt propaganda and "racial rhetoric" for the most part as obstacles to literary excellence and universal acceptance. They eschewed the stereotypes and easy moral solutions of the past. Hence, the personae of the stories by Rudolph Fisher, Zora Neale Hurston, Toomer, and Walrond are neither virtuous "stuffed shirts" created to win the approval of white readers nor stock-in-trade embodiments of racial woes and aspirations. They have human strengths and frailties, are villains as well as heroes. Protest, explicit or implicit, is to be found of course in a number of the poems included here, but there are also many poems in which it either does not appear or has been made subordinate.

Not all the imaginative writing in *The New Negro* is of uniformly high quality. Some of it is flawed by a lingering Victorianism, some of it "arty" or technically gauche. Many of the critical essays, particularly those by Dr. Locke himself, are still required reading and contain valuable insights, although recent events have in some cases given a wry twist to the hopes expressed.

The New Negro articulates the crucial ideas of a generation in rebellion against accepted beliefs and engaged in racial self-discovery and cultural reassessment. It affirms the values of the Negro heritage and expresses hope for the future of the race in this country, stressing the black man's "Americanism." This hope was not shared by Garvey and other nationalists, as we know, and today's black revolutionists repudiate Negro "Americanism" in favor of separatism.

The main thrust of *The New Negro* is clearly integrationist, not separatist. Dr. Locke and most of his collaborators thought of race consciousness and race pride as positive forces making the Negro aware of the true worth of his contributions to American society and helping him to achieve his rightful place in it. His task was interpreted as being twofold. He must be, in Dr. Locke's words, "a collaborator and participant in American civilization," and he must at the same time preserve and implement his own racial traditions.

One is impressed by the optimism which is the prevailing mood of this anthology. That a new day for the Negro has arrived; that he is experiencing a spiritual Coming of Age; that, as Langston Hughes wrote, "we have tomorrow bright before us like a flame"—these are dominant themes. But there are counterthemes as well. We hear them in the protest poems of Claude McKay, for example, and in "The Negro Mind Reaches Out," the essay by W. E. B. DuBois which ends the volume: "And thus again in 1924 as in 1899 I seem to see the problem of the 20th century as the Problem of the Color Line."

Foreword to "A Portfolio of Recent American Poetry"

The making of a poem, like all other creative endeavors, is in the Bahá'í view a spiritual act, a form of worship. 'Abdu'l-Bahá has written: ". . . the acquisition of sciences and the perfection of arts are considered as acts of worship. If a man engages with all his power in the acquisition of a science or in the perfection of an art, it is as if he has been worshipping God in the churches and temples. . . . What bounty greater than this that science should be considered as an act of worship and art as service to the Kingdom of God."*

It seems especially significant that 'Abdu'l-Bahá makes no distinction between "secular" and "religious" art. And we may infer from this that poetry, for example, need not be limited to religious themes (in the usual sense of the term) in order to serve "the Kingdom of God." 'Abdu'l-Bahá sees the creative act as essentially a religious act. The serious artist is involved in a spiritual enterprise. The poet's efforts to master form and technique are in themselves a kind of prayer.

Reprinted with permission from *World Order* 5, no. 3 (Spring 1971):33. Copyright © 1971 by the National Spiritual Assembly of the Bahá'ís of the United States. Hayden wrote this preface for a selection of poetry he made in his capacity as poetry editor of *World Order*.

*Baháu'lláh and 'Abdu'l-Bahá, *Bahá'í World Faith* (Wilmette, Illinois: Bahá'í Publishing Committee, 1943), pp. 377–78. (Hayden's note.— ED.)

The destructive forces at work in the twentieth century, the crises and obsessions of a world in violent transition, account for much that is negative in poetry and the other arts today. Chauvinism, the frenetic quest for novelty, the subordination of the aesthetic to the politically utilitarian—these are, clearly, manifestations of decadence. They are not, however, the only elements discernible. If there is catabolism, there is also anabolism. If there exists a "poetry of despair" and rejection, there is also a poetry that affirms the humane and spiritual. Our attempts at the present time to achieve a new, a larger vision of God, man, civilization give substance to the work of many outstanding poets.

The selections offered our readers in this portfolio attest to the vitality of contemporary American poetry. Several schools or styles are represented. Here are poems that express the malaise and disjunctions of our times as well as poems that reflect personal experience or honor transcendental values. Together, they indicate the variety of modes and voices enriching poetry today.

Foreword to "Recent American Poetry: Portfolio II"

The poems in this, our second *World Order* anthology, represent work by both well-known poets and those who are just beginning to achieve recognition. The selections suggest something of the diversity of modes, forms, and idioms characteristic of contemporary American poetry.

Poetry, always the barometer of its times, today clearly registers the spiritual pressures of this "Age of Anxiety," as W. H. Auden described our period, and it has been strategically affected by them as well. The so-called revolution in American poetry which began in the 1950s was partly initiated by changes in moral outlook and social sensibility; and it helped, in turn, to implement these to some degree. The revolt against tradition has produced by now a poetry with its own conventions and points of emphasis: free or "open" forms, the use of subject matter once regarded as offensive or "unpoetic"; the rejection of the "literary" in favor of the experiential and spontaneous. Although this "new" poetry has not supplanted formal modes (often justifiably criticized as "academic"), it has, nevertheless, modified and in general taken precedence over them.

Reprinted with permission from *World Order* 9, no. 4 (Summer 1975):44–45. Copyright © 1975 by the National Spiritual Assembly of the Bahá'ís of the United States. Hayden wrote this preface for a selection of poetry he made in his capacity as poetry editor of *World Order*.

If the new poetry seems less controversial now than it did two decades ago, it also appears in retrospect to have been less iconoclastic than its partisans boasted. It was, really, less spontaneous combustion than the upsurge of fires kindled in the past. The current belief that poets should be free to write about whatever they choose and that poetry need not conform to academic standards of excellence are almost universally accepted as part of the gospel of "the new, the radical." There is little, if anything, here to refute—and certainly nothing that is novel or daring. Ever since the nineteenth century, poets have been exploring territory once thought better suited to the cultivation of fiction, and their work has encompassed more and more of the quotidian, the psychological, the realistic, and so on. Whitman, Baudelaire, Rimbaud, and Hopkins were among the first to stake out claims which poets since the last century have fully developed. In our own era, the experiments of Ezra Pound, William Carlos Williams, and Charles Olson provided impetus for redefinitions of the nature and function of poetry.

Some of these redefinitions are, of course, open to question. But there is no gainsaying the vigor of our poetry at its best. Kaleidoscopic in its variety, it has tremendous range and flexibility as a medium for expressing all aspects of life and thought. One is aware, moreover, of an emergent world view, a growing world consciousness among our poets. An extremely large body of writing by outstanding foreign poets is available to us in translation, much of it by distinguished American poets. A developing community of feeling which cuts across racial and cultural lines has been encouraged by our familiarity with the work of poets such as Pablo Neruda, Aimé Césaire, Octavio Paz, Leopold Senghor, and Evgeny Yevtushenko. And there is increasing concern with the problems of censorship now confronting artists everywhere. American poetry, itself a significant influence on many poets in other parts of the world, has been open, as perhaps never before, to the influences of cultures and literatures different from our own. The Japanese haiku, the Persian ghazal, African and Eskimo mythology, Chinese philosophy, Indian mysticism—to cite a few examples—have all had definite impact within recent years.

There are, of course, bleak areas of parochialism and pockets of confusion in American poetry today—as in that of every period. One of our most dubious assumptions at present seems to be that the ability to "express oneself" is more important than craftsmanship, style, or aesthetic insight. Indeed, such elements are, from this point of view, synonymous with "elitism." The rejection of "elitist" (bourgeois, genteel) criteria involves not so much the repudiation of tired conventions and official attitudes as it does the abandonment of the very qualities which differentiate poetry from other kinds of experience. An exchange of one set of mediocrities for another has resulted in a species of nonpoetry—verse that is amorphous in structure, trivial in substance, and pretentious. This kind of verse is, more often than not, informed by a crass naturalism and linguistic violence which delude those responsible for it into believing they are "telling it like it is." Yet they have been hailed in some quarters as the "voices of revolution."

But the truly revolutionary poets are always those who are committed to some integrative vision of art and life. Theirs is an essentially spiritual vision which leads to the creation of new forms and techniques, to a new awareness.

"Without vision the people perish."

Foreword to "Anne Frank: The Child and the Legend"

Rosey E. Pool (1905–1971) was a radiant force for human understanding and unity. Writer, scholar, teacher, Bahá'í, she possessed a breadth of heart and mind that made all people her people and all countries her home.

Years before the civil rights movement focused attention on the work of Afro-American poets, Rosey, a native of Holland, was their eloquent advocate, their vigorous campaigner. She had first become aware of this literature in 1925 while a student at the University of Amsterdam, where she did extensive research in the field. When she came to the United States, it surprised, indeed annoyed her to discover that most Negro poets were unknown in their own country, or, if known, were given only a tenuous kind of recognition.

In 1958 she edited the bilingual anthology *I Saw How Black I Was* (published in the Hague as *Ik Zag Hoe Zwart Ik Was*) in collaboration with her brilliant young countryman Paul Breman. She had done much to encourage Breman's interest in Afro-American poets, and he was later to bring out special editions of their work in his Heritage Series, published in London, where both he and Rosey went to live after the Second World War. He began the series with the publication of my *Ballad of Remembrance* in 1962. Rosey's *Beyond the Blues,*

Reprinted with permission from *World Order* 6, no. 3 (Spring 1972): 51–52. Copyright © 1972 by the National Spiritual Assembly of the Bahá'ís of the United States.

one of her most popular anthologies, appeared in London the same year.

In addition to writing, editing, translating, and teaching, Rosey was for many years involved in broadcasting, first in radio in its infant days in Holland and afterwards in television as well. She appeared on both the British and Canadian broadcasting systems and also on many American radio and television programs. She achieved prominence as a radio and television "personality" in Holland.

Rosey visited the United States several times, her first tour made possible by a Fulbright grant. While here she gave poetry readings—she was a superb interpretive reader—lectured, and taught at various schools and colleges, particularly in the South. She eagerly sought out talented young authors, and as a teacher of creative writing she was unstinting in her efforts to help students develop their gifts. She collected aspiring poets and their manuscripts with what seemed to some of us reckless enthusiasm.

Rosey was no self-deluded Lady Bountiful indulging herself in racial "uplift." She approached the work of Negro poets not as material to be manipulated to fit a thesis, but as writing that had its own intrinsic value as well as a universal significance in terms of the worldwide struggle against oppression. Having suffered Nazi persecution, she understood the realities of American race prejudice and identified with its victims. And she knew that the struggle to achieve true human status and the struggle to create art, music, and literature were fundamentally one.

When Hitler invaded Holland, Rosey was put in charge of a Jewish high school. She also joined the Dutch Resistance, exposing herself to danger by taking part in rescue missions. Eventually she and her family were sent to a concentration camp, because by their own naive (as Rosey put it) admission they had originally been Jews, though at the time of the occupation they were Catholics. Rosey's relatives were killed. She herself was subjected to physical and mental tortures that would surely have destroyed her, she told us, but for the divine protection she prayed for and received in the worst moments. She often recalled how she and her fellow prisoners, wishing to pray together in secret yet lacking a common faith, used lines from Negro spirituals instead, because these old songs expressed what they all felt most deeply. Rosey managed to escape from the camp and lived hidden for nineteen months until the Liberation.

In the accompanying article she has left us a tender yet unsentimental memoir of Anne Frank. She was Anne's English teacher in the days before their arrest and internment. And it was Rosey who originally translated Anne's now famous *Diary* into English. I have the impression that she never received proper recognition for this work.

When I first met Rosey, some time in the early sixties, she was not a Bahá'í. She knew about the Faith, of course, evincing openmindedness and a certain amount of sympathy when we discussed it. Subsequently, while on a world tour, she visited Haifa. At the Shrine of the Báb, she said, she underwent a mystical experience of such power that she felt she was *destined* to become a Bahá'í. Upon her return to this country, she made an intensive study of the Writings under the guidance of Mrs. Florence Bagley of Huntsville, Alabama, and came into the Faith. She was then teaching at Alabama A & M. I saw her for the last time when I participated in a literary festival she had organized there. I remember how happy she was. Until her recent death in London she worked ardently for the Bahá'í Faith.

I cherished Rosey as a friend and admired her as one of the most spiritually vital people I have ever known. She affirmed life. She evoked the best in us. She was full of zest and courage to the end.

"Something Patterned, Wild, and Free"

I have been writing for many years now, but my development as a poet has been slow and tortuous, and my failures are more numerous than my successes, owing partly to the fact that I have had to work in defiance of limitations imposed from without while fighting personal demons within. Yet I know that the struggle to exist as a poet at all has given my life its truest definition.

Though I eschew the didactic, I admit to being a poet "with a purpose." Naturally, I want my poetry to stand primarily as poetry. But I want it also to serve God and affirm and honor man, however indirectly. I think of the writing of a poem as a prayer for understanding and perfection—indeed, as a form of worship.

My plans, hopes, expectations regarding future work? For one thing, I should like to write about my personal experiences more directly than I seem to have done in the past. For another, I hope to add to the poems I have already published on themes from Negro history and folklore, because this material interests me and is untarnished by overuse, and because it gives me the chance to reaffirm the Negro struggle as part

From the pamphlet "The New Poetry Scene" which accompanied the recording *Today's Poets: Their Poems—Their Voices*, 4 (FS11004) edited by Stephen Dunning. Copyright © 1967 by Scholastic Records. Reprinted by permission.

of the long human struggle toward freedom. Finally, I want to experiment with forms and techniques I have not used before—to arrive at something really my own, something patterned, wild, and free.

III

Interviews and Conversations

A Conversation During the Bicentennial

The country is getting ready to celebrate the Bicentennial of its founding. What does America mean to you? Are you proud to be an American?

Well, it means a great deal to me, and I want to try to answer that question as carefully as I can. I wouldn't say that I am proud exactly, for I regard racial and national pride as a rather dubious value, as something which tends to be divisive—to exclude. America is home to me, the country in which I can work most effectively. Although, as the poet Claude McKay said, "She feeds me bread of bitterness," I

Reprinted with permission from *World Order* 10, no. 2 (Winter 1975–76):46–53. Copyright © 1976 by the National Spiritual Assembly of the Bahá'ís of the United States. Glenford E. Mitchell, the former managing editor of *World Order,* conducted the interview. Hayden assisted in one stage of the editing of the transcript. There is a biographical note, deleted here, in which Hayden is quoted as saying, "I am a poet who teaches in order to earn a living so that he can write a poem or two now and then. I was born and raised in the slums of Detroit. My family was poor, hard working, with no education. But they wanted me to have an education and sacrificed and helped me to go to college. My roots are really very deep in what I like to call Afro-American folk life." Some internal editorial material is also deleted without indication of ellipses.

have a deep love for my country; I feel very much a part of it despite some sense of alienation. It's an emotional frame of reference for me, and I feel deeply involved with the fate of the country.

What is the meaning of America's past to you?

That calls for a rather complicated answer. I am somewhat history oriented and have thought much and written about certain aspects of our past. The past is for most Americans, unfortunately, rather meaningless. But some of us are aware of it as a long, tortuous, and often bloody process of becoming, of psychic evolution—a process continuing today and, as a result of worldwide stress, gaining in momentum. And it has required, in almost every generation, a clarification, a redefinition of the concepts, principles, abstractions, if you will, which we have believed essential to our development as a nation. The concepts of freedom and democracy, the concepts of the individual and individual rights, even the definition of "human" are different now from what they were two hundred years ago. Slaves and Indians in the eighteenth century, for example, were hardly regarded as human. Consider also the status of women then. We, in our times, are obligated to go on with the process of redefinition. We are still struggling with the evils of our past, but we have also inherited ideals which we are obligated to clarify and implement. Is that too complicated?

We pressed for more comment. Has America fulfilled the promise of its past?

Well, yes and no. I think it's too easy to generalize and say no. I should say as a sort of preface that I don't feel our past is to be honored and revered by restaging the Boston Tea Party or the Battle of Bunker Hill. That seems to me mere jingoism. I should say, perhaps tangentially at this point, that our glorious past was not all that glorious anyway. Imagine the irony of slaves and Indians fighting to free an America which considered them brutes at best, and at worst devils. And how can we overlook the waste and exploitation of human and natural resources in the name of progress and "Manifest Destiny." But to get on with the question you asked, I would say yes, the promise of the past has been fulfilled in significant ways—most significantly in terms of individual freedom. But I hasten to add that freedom is always endangered, always threatened. Many aspects of the promise of the past have never been realized because we have only paid lip service to the ideals of justice and equality and humanity which we claim are fundamental to our way of life. We have allowed reactionaries to subvert us in too many instances.

We wanted Mr. Hayden to elaborate on his reference to reactionary forces.

I don't want to get involved in name calling, but I am thinking of all of those organizations and demagogues that stand in the way of a broader development of our institutions; of those who are opposed to other people and groups of people on the basis of color, religion, national origin, or things of that type; of those who attempt—and today too often succeed—to control and suppress, to destroy in order to shore up a tottering power structure. This is what I mean by reactionary forces: those forces which really do stand in the way of real social and spiritual progress. I think we all know who they are.

Do you love the land?

Indeed, I do. Indeed, I do. I have traveled extensively throughout the country, and I have lived in several different regions of the country. Physically, it's a spectacular country, with everything in it from deserts to the most lush gardens. It's full of dramatic contrasts and is often incredibly beautiful—the Far West, for example, especially San Francisco. I am always impressed with the variety and the individual qualities which the various regions of the country have, and I have tried to write poems about parts of the country I have experienced. It's a very hard thing to do. The land is as varied as the people, and there is no one thing you can say about it. Parts of it are being ruined, as we know, in the name of industrial progress. I find this highly symbolic of our aggressive utilitarianism.

With whom or with what do you identify?

That's really a very hard question. Obviously, I identify with Bahá'ís—and with other artists, and with the kind of people with whom I grew up, poor people, working-class people. I tend to identify with anything which is human, drawing the line of course against those people who are cruel and rapacious and so on. I have a very deep feeling about humanity. I'm not a joiner. I don't get involved with groups. The Bahá'í Faith is about the only organized body I can stand. I cherish my individuality and don't want to be a conformist except (paradoxically) on my own terms. But I care about people, respond to whatever is human. If I didn't feel that way, how could I write? What would I write about?

What grieves you about America?

Oh, there are many things that grieve me. As a matter of fact, it would take me hours to discuss them. But I think that the racial situation grieves me most, because it is so wasteful and frustrating, so vicious and irrational. As an old friend of mine once said, "Races are not important, but people are." We don't have a sense of this in America.

Another thing that deeply grieves me is our worship of power and technology, our failure to honor any kind of spiritual vision. For example, the arts in America exist pretty largely as entertainment. The artist in this country has a kind of marginal existence, and unless he is an entertainer or unless he does something sensational and gets his name in the paper, there doesn't seem to be much place for him. There are no poets in the government that I know of. There are no artists of any kind holding responsible government positions.

One reason for this is that there is a great suspicion and distrust of the arts; and, as I say, since the arts do involve the spiritual and do involve spiritual vision, there is not much concern with that.

I think what it really all comes down to, if you think of the racial situation and the position of the artist in society and you think of our rampant technology—that what it comes down to is wastefulness and exploitation, waste of human and natural resources, and of spiritual resources. This is very terrible, and I think more and more people are feeling this way and that we have got to put an end to it, and the only way we can put an end to it, of course, is to have a brand new vision of what we are.

What would you change in America?

Attitudes. I would hope that we could achieve new concepts of what it is to be human—a new vision of our relationship to God, to one another. Basically, a change of heart. Everything would follow from that. Anything else, it seems to me, is a stopgap measure. Unless there is an absolute, fundamental change in our attitudes toward one another, present evils will continue, will grow worse. A difficult task, this changing of attitudes, but our survival depends on it.

Do you see this fundamental change taking place?

In the minds and hearts of spiritually mature people it is. Many of them seem to be questioning accepted ideas and rejecting old assumptions once considered beyond question. I'd say the various liberation movements are instances of this. Everything is under scrutiny today; everything is in ferment. For there has been a new release of spiritual energy in the world, a galvanizing force which nothing can deter. Bahá'ís know its source to be Bahá'u'lláh. It's impelling all of us toward a new consciousness.

Now it is very difficult to change, and if the change involves some material object or if it involves the damming of a river or putting up of a building, that could be done with no problem. But when it comes to changing attitudes and when it comes to gaining new concepts, it is very difficult. I think that time is running out, and we are being forced to rethink our values and redefine ourselves, our goals, our country, whatever.

Do you think that a redefinition is possible to humanity or at least to America now?

I think so. As a matter of fact, I feel that is what the various liberation groups are all about. As wrong-headed as some of them are, they are still attempting to find new ways of solving problems. The way is being prepared for some kind of a change. We are confronted by terrifying dilemmas which, for their solution, demand a redefinition of ourselves. Redefinition will come about as the result of a renewal of transcendent belief.

How then do you see America's future? Where is America going?

What can I say? I believe what the Bahá'í teachings tell us about the destiny of America. All I can do is have faith. From the Bahá'í Writings we learn that America is to become the spiritual leader of the world. Now if I weren't a Bahá'í, I could hardly conceive of that, because things are so grim, there is so much corruption, there seems to be so little regard for spiritual values, and we have allowed irresponsible power-hungry men to lead us into a kind of labyrinth. Yet negative thoughts aside, one cannot help seeing the potential greatness of this country, once we are a united people. Throughout our history Americans have believed America has a purpose, a peculiar destiny, have believed in what we may call the new-world mystique. The Bahá'í Faith reinforces this idea but cautions us we are going to have to be purged of our weaknesses—our old-world sickness—before we can achieve our appointed task. Isn't America as much a spiritual idea as it is a physical entity or geographical unit?

You were mentioning the need for a change of heart and for adherence to spiritual ideals and so on. Are you referring to a sort of spiritual transcendence?

Yes, I am. How else shall we evolve except through commitment to transcendent values? It's not something which can be programmed, however; it's a matter of individual consciousness and conscience. Consider that in the past Americans have always been dissenters. Americans have never submitted for long to injustice. They have always gone to the defense of the underdog. Even in the days of slavery there were those people, like the Quakers, and there were the great men like Emerson and Thoreau, who laid it on the line and protested. Thoreau spent a night in jail rather than pay taxes to a slave-holding government. This is something which, during this Bicentennial period, we need to remember—that is, we have always been dissenters. There have always been among us people who have some vision of how things ought to be, and they have led the rest of us, the rest of the country, in the right direction. I think that this is true now. There are many voices warning us and exhorting us to live better and be better than we are. So this is something that has been true of America since its inception. If you think of the Indian situation, from the beginning there were those people who wanted to see the Indians treated right, who did not want to rob them and cheat them. It is too easy to generalize and say that America is a great vicious monster. This isn't true. Elements of the monster are certainly among us, but we have always had the people who have challenged tyranny and spoken for the truth.

What would you identify as the destiny of America? What goal are we striving for, sensibly or insensibly?

I make the point in a piece I am writing that we don't really know ourselves, don't know what we are. We are so many different things, and beyond material advancement we don't seem to know what it is we ought to be living for. There are exceptions to this, naturally. But I am straying from the question. To answer it directly, let me say that America seems destined to bring together all the people of the world. The country is already a kind of microcosm, and we are more and more international in outlook.

Let me give you an example. I was recently in San Francisco, and one of the things that impressed me was that San Francisco, like New York, is a very international city. It is possible to meet people from all over the world in either one of those cities. Even though living conditions are certainly not ideal, and the mutual respect among people is not all it should be—despite all that, you have the sense that people live more or less in harmony and that they are interested in one another's culture. There is a kind of mingling of cultures. We stayed, for example, in a Japanese hotel. We didn't feel strange in that hotel, which was a combination of Western and Japanese. I get excited when I think about this because nationalism in any form is one of the evils of our times, and nationalism can only bring more and more antagonism and more and more suspicion amongst people. To come again more directly to the question: History, or events, seem to be pushing us toward internationalism, a world view. The Bahá'í Teachings assure us that America will be an instrument for peace in the future. I think that maybe America is being prepared for that as a result of having all the races, cultures, and nationalities of the world in one way or another in the country.

Does your art relate to America?

Well, I hope it does. My experiences as an American have obviously provided me with themes and determined how I look at life. I have never been a flag-waving patriot, but I profoundly believe in democracy, in the sacredness of the individual, in the dream of freedom for all. I am interested in American history, and I have written on historical themes. This does not mean that, as I have said, I do not find much to deplore, much to be angry about in our society. Thus I have written poems which lament or criticize aspects of America. I am not interested in any form of cultural nationalism, clearly. American life is a point of departure for me into an awareness of the universal.

Looking at the relationship between my art and America from a very different perspective, I do find much in American life which is very exciting and much that is new and untried in the arts. There is great vitality and great energy here, and there is also material which has not yet been used, even by American writers and by American artists. I find all of this very exciting and very challenging.

Do you feel that your poetry is American poetry?

Well, I don't know. A flip answer would be yes, because an American is writing it. Seriously, I have been thinking about this point, about what makes a poem American. I don't know whether American poets know. I once played around with a list of attributes for an American poem, and then I gave it up because I found that the list wasn't very good. Some poets have tried to write *the* American poem. Walt Whitman comes to mind first, for he saw himself as the bard of the American people. Hart Crane wrote about the Brooklyn Bridge, a very American theme. William Carlos Williams, Ezra Pound, and others have explored native themes and idioms. But it is difficult, if not downright impossible, to define American poetry. Maybe, it's a matter of language, the rejection of "literariness" in favor of the colloquial; maybe, a matter of outlook, social vision. The best American poets from Whitman on have very often eschewed the so-called poetic diction and tried to write a poetry that was very close to the English which Americans speak. American poets, I believe, are usually more harshly critical of their country than most other poets are permitted to be. Certainly this is one-up for the United States. Though it may seem immodest on the poets' part, we can't help believing sometimes that we are the conscience of our people. I hope we never lose the freedom to write as we please— though we might. Some of my poems have been censored by textbook committees in the South. Which brings me back to a statement about my own work. Perhaps it is American poetry in that it often reflects my social consciousness, in that I feel free to write out of my own particular kind of awareness. But, to put it bluntly, I don't know what I'm talking about at this point!

What elements in America have been crucial to your artistic identity?

That's difficult to answer without being trite. I have to admit, though, that the racial situation has been strategic. It has both deterred and stultified me, and provided a kind of negative impetus. But that is not the only element. I have given a lot of thought to this, and I see that my struggles to be worthy as a poet and as a man, my own quest for my meaning as an individual have been crucial. Other artists would say much the same thing, for it is extremely difficult, not to say hazardous, to live as an artist in the United States. Poets are marginal people for the most part and always have been. Americans are a pragmatic people. We like to praise the pioneers and talk about the pioneer spirit, but the pioneers and the pioneer spirit had some very negative qualities too. They tended to be utilitarian. If you could eat it, wear it, or use it to build a fire with, it was good; if not, not. I think that every American artist has to struggle for his identity; he has somehow to survive in the midst of indifference and even downright antagonism. Now I'm not asking that there be no struggle. I think that some sort of struggle is necessary to the artist as it is to any human being, but there is a kind of puritanism in American life, a carry-over from the past which distrusts the arts. As I said earlier, we tend to confuse art and entertainment, and we don't read poetry, for one thing. We have very little knowledge of poetry. There are many fine poets writing today, and the average well-educated person doesn't know who they are and doesn't really care. I won't go into the whys and wherefores of that, because that's a very long story. But I think that this creates certain problems for the poet, and I might say that I think the situation is better today than when I was a young person trying to be a poet. There seem to be more outlets and a little more interest than there was then.

But I want to get back to the question. Crucial in my development has been the coming to grips with myself, my own soul, if you will, with my own realities as they have been revealed to me through my dedication to poetry and, yes, through religion. I have had to struggle to be a poet, and in some ways the struggle has been good for me. I am rather glad sometimes that it has been difficult, for it has given me a strength, a toughness of will, I might not have otherwise had. I have gained some sort of perspective that allows me the freedom to go my own way these days, despite the demands made upon my life and art by those who want me to "submit to ideology," political and racial.

What elements of American poetry are universal and why?

I think that, with some exceptions, most of it seems to have a universal appeal. Russian poets and Latin American poets are heavily influenced by American poetry. So also are some of the poets in oriental countries, Japan, for example. There are some American poets whose work seems overspecialized, geared to ethnic or political criteria; but, as I suggested in an article I wrote for *World Order,* many American poets today have a world view.* There is considerable universality in American poetry, and, ironically, this is often criticized as undesirable by those who want nationalistic rhetoric, and so forth. In the past a great poet like Whitman, while he wanted to be *the* poet of the American people, hoped that everybody was going to read him and know his work. Of course, his hope was never realized; nevertheless, he was a cosmic poet, and we honor him today for his attempt. Many of us would hope that we too might achieve a degree of universality.

---

*World Order (Summer 1975). (Hayden's note.) Reprinted on pp. 68–70.—ED.

"A Certain Vision"

I heard a story recently about a high school student in Columbia, a boy who had written a poem that was going to be included in his class anthology. He said, "Yes, you can use it, but don't use my name. My daddy would kill me if he knew I was writing poetry."

Oh, yeah, yeah.

You have said that your family was poor and hardworking, with no education, but that they sacrificed and helped you to go to college. How did they feel about your choice of profession?

Well, they certainly didn't interfere with it. They didn't understand too well what I was doing, but they wanted me to get an education. They wanted me to use my talent in some way, and they never objected to my writing poetry. They didn't know very much about it, as I say. They knew that I wanted to be a writer, and they never objected to it. They were con-

---

An interview with Robert Hayden by Richard Layman, which originally appeared in *Conversations with Writers 1,* edited by Richard Layman (copyright © 1977 Gale Research Company; reprinted by permission of the publisher) Gale, 1977, pp. 157–79. Hayden was interviewed on 7 May 1977 in Columbia, South Carolina, where he received an Honorary Degree of Doctor of Letters from Benedict College. Hayden approved a transcript of the interview before its final editing.

cerned that I find some sort of work to support myself and all that. But there was never any difficulty at home about my writing.

When did you decide that you were going to be a poet? Sounds like you started quite early.

I did start quite early. I learned to read before I went to public school, and I began trying to write poems and stories and plays while I was down in the grades. I told about this the other night in my talk at the Library of Congress.* I remember that when I was in the grades the teacher gave us a list of words for spelling and told us to put the words into sentences. I made up a story out of the words instead of just putting them into sentences. When I was in what was called in those days intermediate school, which today we call junior high school, I was trying to write poetry. By the time I got into high school I felt that I wanted to be a poet, and I was devoting all my time to it. I was reading poetry all the time and trying to write it, not knowing very much about it and not really having too much encouragement, but feeling very deeply that I wanted to write in that way, that I wanted to write poetry.

Was there a place to publish in your high school?

I had a short story in the school annual, and I had a brief sketch in the school paper. In both instances, they were not poetry. But I did have work in the school annual and the school paper.

So when you went to college, you knew what you were going to major in; you knew what you were going to do?

Well, yes and no to that. I wasn't quite sure about myself as a poet. I loved poetry, and I was trying to write it and always

_____
*From *The Life: Some Remembrances,* 3 May 1977. Reprinted on pp. 17–27.—ED.

was reading it. But if I must be honest, I didn't have the kind of faith in myself that other young people seemed to have had. Certainly the student poets that I work with all have faith in themselves, and I didn't have that kind of faith. But I did like English, and I had done very well in English courses in high school. When I went to college, interestingly enough, I majored in foreign languages, with a minor in English. I had poems in the college paper. I went to what was then the Detroit City College; later it became Wayne State University. I had poems in the school paper and I came to be known as a poet. I never had any courses in creative writing as an undergraduate student.

Were they available?

There was just one, as I recall. Somehow or other my schedule never permitted me to take that one course in creative writing. But I did do some writing in my freshman composition courses and in other English courses. Though it wasn't poetry, the instructors thought I showed talent, and occasionally I would read a paper in front of the class, you know, that kind of thing.

You said you were reading a lot. What were you reading, do you recall?

Well, as a child I read, I suppose, mostly the things that most children read. Even though my family was poor and completely uneducated—that is my foster parents; my foster parents reared me—my own mother had an interest in books and so on. She was living in Buffalo, and from time to time she would send me books. I remember she sent me *Black Beauty*, the story of a horse, and *Beautiful Joe*, the story of a cur. Strangely enough, I read *Uncle Tom's Cabin* and I read *Robinson Crusoe*.

Later on, when I was in high school, I was in the sight conservation class because my sight was so very poor that I was taken out of the regular homeroom and put into this very special homeroom where our reading was supervised. We were not permitted to read small type, and we wrote on manila sheets of paper and used big, thick pencils—to this day I'm addicted to big, thick, black pencils and so on. But one of my sight-saving teachers used to read my assignments in English to me, and I remember that we were to read a book and report on it. I chose George Eliot's *Romola*. That had a tremendous influence on me, remember I was in high school. In the first place, I learned words that I had never known before. To this day I can remember how intrigued I was with the word *loggia*, and the names of things, like the "Ponte Vecchio," and so on. I lived in that book; I just loved it.

And then later on—I guess I was out of high school or in my last year, I've forgotten—I read Hawthorne's *The Marble Faun;* and I read *The Last Days of Pompeii;* and I read Papini's *The Story of Christ;* I read *Toby Tyler;* or, *Ten Weeks with a Circus.* And those books stayed with me. Hawthorne's *The Marble Faun*—I've tried to read it since; I tried to read it several years ago and I didn't get very far with it. But I was about seventeen or eighteen when I read those books.

Again, I lived in *The Marble Faun;* I thought it was a marvelous thing—the atmosphere and the poetry in the novel and the mystery that Hawthorne worked out there in which one of the characters looks like Donatello's *Marble Faun.* He doesn't have the pointed ears like the marble faun and maybe he is, if not evil, at least amoral or something. Well, that and *The Last Days of Pompeii.* I loved those books, partly because they took me completely out of the environment that I lived in, and they appealed to my imagination, because they were full of strange and wonderful things that I'd had no direct experience with.

Brendan Gill has said he thought that all of a man's reading was done by the time he was thirty; that is, all the reading that would influence his development.

Well, I don't know whether I agree with that entirely. I've read books after that period that meant a great deal to me. I think some of Henry James's novels, particularly the novellas, like *The Aspern Papers* and *The Turn of the Screw.* Those meant a great deal to me, also. But I think I know what Brendan Gill means: that the books you read before you're thirty have a different kind of influence upon you, different from the influence that books after that have on you, because they help somehow to shape your sensibilities. They help somehow to stimulate your imagination. In a sense they help to form, perhaps, your aesthetic sense, and they help to form the particular kind of creative mind-set that you're going to have later on. So maybe that's true.

Who were the poets that you thought highly of in that period?

Oh, well, in that period, I think that I could certainly name them right off. Countee Cullen, whom I read with almost bated breath. I just thought he was one of the greatest poets that I'd ever heard of. And Carl Sandburg and Edna Millay and—oh, about the time I was ready to go to college, Elinor Wylie and Orrick Johns; some of these poets are completely forgotten now. Orrick Johns and Langston Hughes and the whole—I discovered the poets of the Harlem Renaissance quite by accident. I remember going through the library and getting the volume edited by Alain Locke called *The New Negro.* I discovered those poets and I went to the library and got individual volumes by each of them.

I could say that in that period, oh, when I was about ready to go to college—after high school there was an interim period when I didn't have the money to go to college and I was just hoping and, you know, trying various things, odd jobs now and then, but mostly reading and trying to be a poet—at that time I'd go to the library and get out all the anthologies, and I just knew everybody almost. But the poets I've mentioned I think were my favorites. Of course, I haven't mentioned Lola Ridge—Lola Ridge, who wrote *Firehead* and a book of poems called *Dance of Fire,* and *Ghetto,* and *Sun-Up* and so on. I discovered her about that time. I read *Firehead* and thought it was one of the great poems.

From what you've said you seem to have had a taste in nineteenth-century romantic novels and contemporary 1920s poetry.

Yes.

That seems a strange mixture.

It was a strange mixture. I did read some twentieth-century novels in the period we're speaking of. I read the chief popular stuff. I loved Sax Rohmer. I read the Fu Manchu stories.

Edgar Wallace?

No, not so much Edgar Wallace. I read Sax Rohmer's Fu Manchu, that was my great . . . I obviously, see, have always had this feeling for the exotic, without really being conscious of it. And I used to read all the Fu Manchu I could get my hands on. Then, of course, I read a couple of volumes of the Tom Swift stories, and I read Langston Hughes; of course, I was in college then. I read Langston Hughes's *Not Without Laughter.* I don't think the novel has been reprinted, but it was a novel about a woman who became a well-known blues singer and so on. And I read Carl Van Vechten's *Nigger Heaven,* and things like that. But I tended to read poetry for the most part.

Oh, I must tell you this, which will surprise you. While I don't seem to have read a great many novels, I became interested in Eugene O'Neill. And I read everything; I read everything. I remember so well O'Neill's *Mourning Becomes Electra* coming to Detroit, and how I longed to go and see that play. And before that time *Strange Interlude* had come to Detroit. I simply didn't have the money to go and see either of those plays, but I had read them. I'd go to the library and just get out all of Eugene O'Neill and read them. I don't know what kind of influence it had on me, but I did go through an O'Neill period.

You said you thought of yourself as a poet. Did you have any contact at all with professional poets, published poets?

No, not until I met Langston Hughes.

When was that?

I met him in the thirties. I guess I was still in college. I have a good memory, but today dates are eluding me. But this was in the thirties when I met Langston Hughes. He was the first recognized poet I ever met. He had come to Detroit to see a production of one of his plays that a dramatic group in Detroit was putting on. I was in the play, and I asked the director, Elsie Rocksboro, who was a close friend of Langston Hughes, to arrange for me to meet him. And she did. We had lunch together and I did what young poets always do; I showed him some of my poems. He wasn't terribly enthusiastic. He thought that they were too much like other people's poems, which I'm sure they were at that time. And he pointed out that I needed to find my own voice; I needed to find something. I needed to work and find what my own voice was and do something that was more individual, because some of my poems were too like those of other poets. I was a little crestfallen, I guess, but I was very excited to meet this poet, who at that time was, you know, very famous and sort of glamorous. We read about him traveling all over the world, and he was having plays produced, and he had been one of the bright stars of the Harlem Renaissance; so it was really quite exciting to meet him. Then when I went to Harlem— after I was married, my wife and I went to Harlem one summer.

About when was that?

This was 1940. No, it was 1941; it was the second year of our marriage. She was studying music at Juilliard, and her uncle had been in college with Countee Cullen. So Erma called Mr. Cullen. He remembered her, because he had known her when she was a very young person, and he invited us to come out and visit him. Again I was enthralled, because I had read all of Countee Cullen's poetry, and I was delighted to meet him. I remember that he was very affable, and he was interested in me. There was a poem of mine that he liked—I had had a book published by this time. There's a poem in my early book *Heart-Shape in the Dust* that's called "The Falcon," and he wanted me to read it. He had a copy of the book—maybe I had sent it to him or took him one, I've forgotten now. And I read "The Falcon." I was very flattered to think that he wanted, you know, to hear a poem from me.

We didn't talk very much about writing poetry, about the craft of poetry or anything of the kind. It was really a social evening. The widow and the sister of Rudolph Fisher were also at Countee Cullen's house, and there was some talk about the Harlem Renaissance and the Negro movement. I recall that Cullen wanted my wife to play a Chopin étude. My wife is a pianist, and she did. It was a pleasant evening. Afterwards, when I looked back on it, I felt that it had been awfully genteel, you know, really very genteel. But it was a chance to meet Countee Cullen, and that was the first and only time that I saw him. I heard from him after that, but I didn't see him anymore before his death.

Heart-Shape in the Dust *was published in 1940.*

That's right.

How did that come about?

Well, that was a local venture.

The Falcon Press?

The Falcon Press, yes. Louie Martin was the editor of the Negro weekly, *The Michigan Chronicle.* I was working part-time on the newspaper and he became interested. He knew that I wrote poetry and he had a certain amount of faith in me, so he decided that he would bring out a book. He told me to get my work together and he'd publish it, and he did. He organized a little company called The Falcon Press, and he brought out *Heart-Shape in the Dust* in 1940. It was what you would imagine: it was the work of a young poet. Of course, I wasn't all that young when it was published, to be sure; what was I, about twenty-seven or so. But it was the work of a young poet, and there are echoes of other poets in it. It was full of, you know, protest poems, and it was full of poems that were primarily concerned with racial themes. It did quite well. The book seemed to move, and today I understand that people are willing to pay, oh, five or six dollars for a copy of it.

Five or six?

Well, maybe more, because you see at that time, back in 1940, I think it was something like $1.50. Some people have advertised for copies and I think perhaps it's worth more than five or six dollars today. I threatened at one time to round up all the copies that were extant and burn them, but I haven't done that. But *Heart-Shape in the Dust* was a young poet's work, and it did get some serious attention. I remember it got a small review in the old *New York Herald Tribune.* People who knew poetry seemed to know something about it. There are several people now who are writing doctoral dissertations or studies of one kind or another on my poetry. They all go back to that book, and they try to assure me that it's not as bad as I think it is.

At that time were you teaching at the University of Michigan?

No. At that time I was on the Writers' Project. When I got married in 1940, I had been on the Writers' Project for a couple of years. I was doing various things; I was sort of doing part-time work at the *Michigan Chronicle* office, and by 1940 I was trying very hard to be a writer. I felt myself to be a poet and was trying to write and trying to learn as much as I could about it. I left the Writers' Project and went on to another project, the Historical Record Survey, and I was fired from that because the WPA projects were winding up and they were getting rid of people; so I found myself without a job. My wife was teaching in the Detroit public school system and she, being rather advanced in her thinking, didn't see why I shouldn't, since I didn't have a job, stay home and write and not worry about it. But oh, I couldn't do that. I was just worried sick because I didn't have a job. But in 1941 we decided that we would leave Detroit and I would go back to the University of Michigan and get my master's degree. And so by 1940 I was married and I had a book published, and then the next year I went to the University of Michigan.

That's when I met my third poet, and that was W. H. Auden. He was teaching at the university; he was teaching a course in the analysis of poetry. He was accepting a few students and I was able to get into his class. That was a marvelous experience. Yes, he was eccentric and odd, but I sort of cherished that. I'm really becoming more and more alarmed by the fact that so many poets now are good academicians in gray flannel suits. But Auden certainly wasn't like that. He was a little awe-inspiring. We all had read his books, you know. We knew that he was brilliant.

When his class began I remember the first day sitting in class really frightened, because I thought, "If he calls on me what will I say?" He was absolutely brilliant. He would quote poems in the original German, and he would quote Latin verses—the range of his learning, the breadth of his knowledge was just extraordinary. He really did inspire us in a sense. His teaching I guess was pretty . . . oh, he would never have won any prizes for pedagogy. But somehow or other he stimulated us to learn more about poetry and even to search ourselves. He made us aware of other literatures, and he made us aware of poetry in a way that we never would have been had it not been for him.

So it was a marvelous experience and, of course, I had a few pleasant personal experiences with him. He read some of my poems. There were some that he liked very much, and some he didn't like at all. The ones he liked he said were poems that were like algebra, in which you were solving for X. He said that was always the best kind of poetry, whereas there were other poems that were like arithmetic: you add them up and get the sum and that's all there is to it. In the other kind of poetry you have to work; you have to try to find the unknown; you have to work for it and so on. I have remembered that ever since he said it.

He came to see my daughter when she was born. Of course, this was a year or so afterwards—after he had left the campus. But he did drop in to see my daughter. He was eager to see what she looked like, and so he looked down at her in her crib. I've told her, "You must remember always W. H. Auden came to look at you." He helped me to get a job in the library. He was friends with the librarian there, Dr. Rice, who later on was the chairman of the English department, and he spoke to Dr. Rice and he got me a job in the library. He was interested in seeing that I got my poems published. He was a wonderful person. And then years later he and I read together at Columbia University.

So you maintained the relationship with him until his death?

Not really. We were aware of each other—rather I should put it the other way round, he was sort of aware of me. After I had a New York publisher, the publisher would send him copies of my books. William Meredith has told me, I don't know what the occasion was, that Auden spoke rather warmly of me and said that he hoped that, oh, I don't know, some prize or some fellowship or something would come my way. Of course, later on I guess it did.

I didn't see him for a very, very long time, and then in 1968 or '69, I think it might have been '69, we were asked to read together at the McMillin Theatre at Columbia University. I had heard that he liked the poem of mine in *Selected Poems* published in '67, the poem called "Witch Doctor." So that night at the McMillin Theatre I read "Witch Doctor" for him. I read first, then he read afterwards. And we did have a chance to talk before the program began. We talked about his years at the University of Michigan, and his coming to see my daughter, and so on. But we were by no means close. We didn't keep in touch, but the following year I was invited to his birthday party. I was in New York and I went to, I guess it was, his sixty-fifth birthday party. And that was the last time I saw him alive.

You got your master's degree from the University of Michigan and taught at the University of Michigan for two years, before you went to Fisk.

Yes. I taught there from—what was it—'44 to '46. I had been a student with advance standing for, oh, two or three years at Michigan, and so I piled up a lot of hours. But it only took me about a year to finish up everything for my master's. And in 1944 I became a teaching fellow in English there.

During this time were you publishing in little magazines?

Yes. I had a few poems published here and there. In 1942 I won the Hopwood Award for poetry at the University of Michigan. And I had some poems published in magazines. Also in about 1946 I had a poem, "Middle Passage," which now has become a well-known poem, that appeared in Edwin Seaver's *Cross Section*. And then I had a poem in the *Atlantic Monthly* in the forties, "Frederick Douglass," which is the other poem that's become very well known. I didn't have a great many poems appearing in magazines. I didn't have all that much time to write. I was a teaching fellow and I had all sorts of responsibilities and so on, and that cut into my writing time.

But I've always had to struggle to write. I've always found it difficult to keep my teaching going and keep my other responsibilities going and write too. I've really had to struggle to get anything out. I think it's partly due to the kind of temperament that I've had. I guess maybe I had so much struggle in my life that . . . I don't know how to say it. Most of the writers that I admire are able to rise above difficulties of one kind or another. Yet, I always find it very hard to, you know, carry on and keep my work going if other things are on my mind, or if I have other obligations. So that has been a problem for me.

You said in an interview in World Order *magazine that was pub-
lished about a year ago that you're a poet who teaches in order to earn
a living so that he can write a poem now and then.* Sounds like you
resent teaching.*

Oh, I don't resent teaching, but I don't love it. I never have
loved it, and I've always been a good teacher. I'm a very
conscientious teacher and also I care about my students. I try
to give them a full measure. But I feel always in conflict,
partly because until recently I've had to teach rather heavy
loads. There was a time in my life when I was teaching fifteen,
sixteen hours a semester and trying to write. And, you know,
it was almost impossible to live as a poet. So I don't know,
maybe I do resent teaching. I know that William James admit-
ted that he had never liked teaching, though he had been an
excellent teacher. I would just say that I've always found it
difficult, and it has always caused conflicts. I've tried to do an
honest job. I've never shortchanged the students in order to
do my own work. But there has always been a great conflict
between my academic chores and my own creative life.

*When you went to Fisk was it as far from Detroit to Nashville as it
would seem?*

Indeed, it was. When I went to Fisk, I had never lived in the
South. I had had very little experience with the South. And
when I went to Fisk in 1946, I knew that a brand new chapter
in my life was beginning and that I was in for an experience
or experiences which I had never had before. My first couple
of years there were extremely difficult for my wife and for
me, and I can't say that we adjusted. We never did adjust to it.
I think it would have been a mistake to adjust to it, but we
came to know how to handle it. We found that it was possible
to form relationships with people of goodwill who did not

---

*World Order (Winter 1975–76). Reprinted on pp. 79–89.—Ed.

have the traditional prejudices. And we found people interested in the arts, people interested in music, and in dance and poetry and so on. And this made a difference.

But we had many difficulties there, because, first of all, we didn't want our daughter to go to a segregated school. We had never gone to one and we didn't want her beginning her education under those circumstances. What we did, of course, was rather drastic. My wife took her to New York, and we put her in a progressive school. My wife was interested in working with modern dance as an accompanist and so on, and even toured with the dance company. I think that it was a blessing, it was a very mixed blessing. Eventually we found that being a divided family was no good for any of us. I went to New York for a year—I took leave from Fisk and went to New York for a year. Then at the end of that year, we came back to Nashville, and my daughter went to the regular public school.

Was it segregated?

Yes, yes. It was segregated. But we felt that—well, two things were influential there. One was that we felt that a great deal of harm was being done by—to her—by the fact that we were a divided family. She didn't quite understand it, you know, at first.

How old was she?

Oh, she was, what, four, five, something like that. And we also felt when we brought her back that she had some background and we could certainly offset some of the harm that might be done to her in the segregated schools. That was a very, very difficult time for us.

Sounds as if you've paid a rather heavy price, emotional and otherwise, to . . .

Indeed, we did.

To teach at Fisk. Why?

Well, for one thing it was very difficult to find a position in another university. Also, I'll go back to this point later, I think I felt that there was a certain amount of good that I could do at Fisk. I found, of course, that Fisk was a pretty sophisticated school and there was certainly nothing . . . well, it wasn't a backwoods institution, let us say. But I think, perhaps, I felt that I could be of some service to the young people there. The other point that I just touched on a moment ago is that in the forties and fifties it was very difficult for an Afro-American to move from one of the schools in the South to a school like Michigan or Harvard or Yale. It's much easier now, but at that time it was very, very difficult. I was at one point in my life considered for a teaching position at the University of Chicago. I was even invited to the university to talk with the various deans—I've forgotten now just what the setup there was. And I was hoping that I was going to get out of the South, you see, and go to teach at the University of Chicago. But it didn't happen. It was very difficult in those days for us to move from the Afro-American schools into the other schools, and that was one reason that we stayed where we were. Jobs were hard to come by.

When you were first describing the move from Detroit to Nashville you kept referring to "it," the pressures of the "it." What did you mean by "it"? More than simple prejudice, I assume.

Oh, well, yes. It was certainly the racial situation, which in Nashville wasn't as bad as it was in some other places in the South, but it was bad enough. The buses were segregated; the schools were segregated; drinking fountains were segregated; and so on. Fisk was kind of an oasis and in the Fisk area, in the Fisk neighborhood, one didn't encounter too much prejudice. As a matter of fact, black and white faculty members lived in the same neighborhood and socialized together and so on, and our children played together and all that kind of thing. But the racial situation in the South was of paramount importance to us because it did pretty much limit us: limit the kind of experiences that we could have, limit the kind of things that we could do, limit opportunities in every single way. There was a time, for example, when I never went to movies in the South, because in order to go to the movie you had to enter the theater through an alley and then go up and sit in what we used to call the buzzard's roost, a Jim Crow balcony. So I never went to the movies in Nashville. And even some stores downtown were unpleasant to shop in. The clerks would call Afro-American people by their first names, whether they really knew them or not. And it wasn't out of a gesture of friendliness, it was a way of telling us that we were not on the same level with the other customers.

And then, too, there was a kind of provincialism in the South. People tended to entertain themselves at home to socialize, not to be so much aware of the larger world, not to be so much interested in, oh, the things that we cared about—modern art, and modern dance, and all this kind of thing. There wasn't so much interest in that. Going to live there meant that we had to . . . we experienced something different from what we had had in the North.

You stayed at Fisk quite a long time, twenty years.

Yeah, more than twenty years, just about twenty-two years.

What was your role there? Were you a poet-in-residence or were you . . .

Not at all, no. I guess I started out as assistant professor of English, and then I became an associate, and then about the time I was ready to leave, I became a full professor. And I taught eighteenth-century literature and I taught creative writing and I taught Afro-American literature and I taught all sorts of things. I was advisor to the student publication, *The Herald.* I worked rather closely with young people who were writing and who were members of my creative writing class, and who were working on *The Herald.* Later on I worked with the Fisk newspaper, *The Fawn.* I was a regular member of the English department and I did what instructors in English would do.

Your second book of poetry. The Lion and the Archer, *was published right after you came to Nashville.*

Yes. I had a Rosenwald Fellowship, and while I was on fellowship I worked on that book with Myron O'Higgins and it was kind of a—it was a far cry, I think, from *Heart-Shape in the Dust.* I was trying to write in a way that I had not written before.

What way is that?

Oh, I can't really describe it. I did go through a period in the forties that I call my baroque period, a period in which my poems were rather heavily ornamented. But I shouldn't say ornamented, because ornamentation sort of connotes the idea that you don't really need it, you know, that it's something that you can do without. But I'll tell you, the kind of imagery and the kind of texture that I tried to create in my poems was different and was what I call baroque. It was more involved, for one thing, and more heavily symbolic, I think, too. I lean toward symbolism anyway. I guess I was trying to work toward something more or less metaphysical, and I was trying to get away from the straight-forward . . . well, I guess I was trying to get away from protest and from poems that were pretty much restricted in theme to racial matters.

This seems a bit odd, too, in light of what you've just said about the shock of moving to Nashville.

Well, I wanted to—as a matter of fact, I did write about the South, and I did write my reactions to it. But I guess I wanted to approach those things as an artist and not as a propagandist, because by this time I had really begun to change in the way I approached these racial matters. I'm just repeating myself, but I guess I'll have to so I can get on to the next point. I wanted to deal with the new experiences; I wanted to, and I wanted to exteriorize and objectify for myself my feeling and so on. But, by this time I was trying to do it, as I say, as a poet and not as a propagandist. The technique or the how was as important to me as the what, you know, or the subject matter.

The book was published in the Counterpoise Series. How did it come about?

Well, Counterpoise was a group endeavor. Some of my students and I got together and decided that we wanted to do something to encourage creative writing at Fisk, and we also wanted to encourage Afro-American writers in general. Again, we wanted to get away from the blatantly propagandistic, and we wanted to get away from the out-and-out protest poem, and we were trying in a sense to make an opportunity for ourselves. Again, this is the forties, and it seemed to me that in the forties there was a great deal going on in the arts, but Afro-Americans, unlike today, were being pretty much ignored. We wanted to do something a little different and encourage one another to do something that was a little off the beaten track. We wanted to encourage people to get away from the obvious poetry that dealt with race and so on. And we wanted to encourage the avant-garde and the experimental—not, of course, that we did it, but we did launch our little movement with the publication of *The Lion and the Archer*. And that's really what the Counterpoise is all about.

We published a little statement; we published a little manifesto. I've forgotten most of the things that we said, but we did get some attention. Sterling Brown wrote a critical article that appeared in one of the Afro-American journals about Counterpoise and *The Lion and the Archer* quite awhile after the series was launched. We wanted to bring out a series of booklets that would be published more or less on a subscription basis. We didn't get too far with it, because it was never all that well worked out.

We published two or three booklets and then we didn't

publish any more. I guess we published four altogether, because as late as '67, or thereabouts, I brought out a group of Margaret Danner's poems, a little collection called *To Flower,* and I called it Counterpoise. I suppose if I were ever to publish another little pamphlet of poems for anybody I'd call it Counterpoise, you know, six or seven or whatever it is. I like the name, and also the idea of encouraging the experimental and the avant-garde still appeals to me. But that's how Counterpoise came about: a group of us got together and sort of drew up a little manifesto. We raised a little money to publish the first booklet and then after that, I guess, I paid for all of them.

Your next book of poetry was Figures of Time, *again published in Nashville, this time by Hemphill Press in 1955.*

Well, that's still in the Counterpoise Series, though.

Oh, is it?

Yes, that was the third. By that time Counterpoise was not—we had never had a very definite structure and all that, but by this time Counterpoise was the name I was giving to a series of things that I hoped to publish and so on. And the Hemphill Press had done them from the very first. The Hemphill Press was the name—or is, they're still in existence—the name of the printers. They were terribly interested in what we were doing and they used to work with me on designing the booklets and getting the special kinds of paper and all the rest of it, because I've always been crazy about beautifully printed books. And these booklets were rather nicely done. We designed them very carefully with the assistance of the Hemphills.

By this time it seems that you certainly had a considerable influence on your students. What was your influence on American poetry?

Oh, none, almost none. Somebody came to Fisk to give a lecture once and said to me, "You have the best underground reputation of any poet in America." And I said, "I wish it would surface," you know, "I wish it would surface." Yes, by this time I had had poems in anthologies and I had won a Rosenwald Fellowship and I had gotten the Ford Foundation Grant for traveling and writing in Mexico. And I had had poems in anthologies that Langston Hughes and Arna Bontemps brought out. I had bits and pieces scattered here and there, and I had the Counterpoise booklets. But it was a long, long time before I could get a publisher interested in a regulation-sized book of poetry.

And at this time people knew that I was a poet. As I say, I had come to be known, to some extent. I didn't get very many readings. My students didn't care all that much about it. Some of them in my creative writing courses were sort of interested that I was a poet. But, you know, I was first of all their teacher, and they didn't even think that I had the real sensibilities and all of a poet. They really didn't. Maybe one or two did, but for the most part, I was their instructor, and occasionally maybe I wrote poetry. As a matter of fact, years after I had left Fisk some of my students said, "Well, you know, I really was surprised after I left Fisk when I heard about you. I was really surprised to know that you really were a serious poet." You see, your students don't . . . I was working at this time and writing as much as I could and when I could. And I had received some recognition, but I was still kind of struggling to establish myself as a poet.

Your next book was published in London. That seems odd.

Well, that was *A Ballad of Remembrance.* My work was known abroad and there was a lovely, lovely person Rosey Pool—who's now dead—a Dutch woman, who had done a great deal of work in American Negro poetry. As a matter of fact, I guess back in the twenties, maybe, when she was a student at a Dutch university, she had been doing research and writing papers, you see, on Afro-American poetry. During the war—she told us this after she came to the United States for a visit—Afro-American poets were quite well known and their works were read a great deal by people who were involved in the underground struggle against Fascism, because they identified with our freedom struggle here and so on.

Paul Breman originated the Heritage series in England. My book, *A Ballad of Remembrance,* was the first in the series. He was a kind of protégé—I guess I shouldn't say that because if Paul Breman hears that he will be mad—but he was a young friend of Rosey Pool's and he was interested in Afro-American poets and poetry. She stimulated his interest, and really whetted his appetite, by giving him books to read and so on and so forth. So he became interested and wanted to publish the work of Afro-American poets, and he did so by launching the Heritage series in London in 1962. He aimed to bring out rather beautiful limited editions of the work of poets that he admired. And he brought out quite a few of these. Then ten years later, in 1972, he brought out my little book, *The Night-Blooming Cereus.* It was kind of a celebration or commemoration of the tenth anniversary of the Heritage series.

I'd like to talk a little bit about the Bahá'í faith.

Yes.

You've said that you're not an organization person and that the only organization that you have much cared about is the Bahá'í faith.

Yes.

When did you convert?

I was a Baptist and when I went to Ann Arbor to work with Auden and started working toward my master's, my wife and I met Bahá'ís on the campus and we went to study groups—that's how you become a Bahá'í; you're not born a Bahá'í. You are required to learn about the faith, to study it, and then to make up your mind whether you want to be a Bahá'í or not. And when we went to Ann Arbor in 1941, we met the Bahá'ís. My wife went to the study groups more often than I did, and she still does, for that matter. She became a Bahá'í first. I made some study of it, and I went to study groups and decided that it was the truth, that it answered a lot of questions that I had never had answers for up to that time. And I became a Bahá'í.

You're now very much involved with World Order *magazine.*

Yes, yes. I'm poetry editor of *World Order* magazine. I don't do as much writing for the magazine as I would like to, but I do some. I'll be working on essays and poems, too, for it. And I'm very happy to be able to do it because one of the attractive features of the Bahá'í faith to me as a poet, or would-be poet or whatever, is that in the writings of Bahá'u'lláh, the prophet of the faith, it's clearly stated that the work of the artist—and by artist I mean anyone engaged in the art of poetry or whatever—the work of the artist is considered a form of service to mankind and it has spiritual significance. If the work is done with great sincerity and devotion and, of course, with knowledge, you know, then it is considered really a form of worship and a form of service to mankind.

I think that today when so often one gets the feeling that everything is going downhill, that we're really on the brink of the abyss and what good is anything, I find myself sustained in my attempts to be a poet and my endeavor to write because I have the assurance of my faith that this is of spiritual value and it is a way of performing some kind of service. Indeed, I feel that very deeply now—I'm not praising my own poetry; I don't mean that I think my poetry is of all that great a consequence to the world—but what I do mean to say is that there is a certain vision of the world that I have. I believe in the essential oneness of all people and I believe in the basic unity of all religions. I don't believe that races are important; I think that people are important. I'm very suspicious of any form of ethnicity or nationalism; I think that these things are very crippling and are very divisive. These are all Bahá'í points of view, and my work grows out of this vision. I have the feeling that by holding on to these beliefs and giving them expression in my work, not always directly—most of the time not directly—at least I'm doing something to prepare, maybe, for a new time, for a new world. And so I guess this is what I mean when I say that maybe I'm doing some sort of service, because at least I'm not going along with the crowds, that is, trying to divide and exploit.

I was going to ask who you wrote to, who your audience was. I suppose in some ways you just answered that.

Yes. For a long time, I guess, I wrote for myself and for a few friends. I have a sort of sense of audience today, because it surprised me to know that my work was so well known throughout the country—I'm not being falsely modest, I really have been surprised to know that it has been read in so many courses in Afro-American literature and in just general English courses throughout the country. I have some sense, I guess, of an audience. I think, really, without being dramatic or, you know, being rhetorical, I guess I write for people, really. I guess I have the feeling that people of discernment, people of goodwill will read the stuff. I don't know.

I get the impression that particularly since you left Fisk, and particularly in the last maybe fifteen years or so, that you've become much more a public poet in the sense that you have been serving short terms as poet-in-residence at various places and that you have been doing a good many more readings and that sort of thing. To what extent does that ironically hinder you as a poet? Is it part of a poet's responsibility to make himself personally visible?

Up to a point, I think, it's the poet's responsibility, but you've hit on something that is very important. A poet—any artist—but a poet, anybody using words, has to be very careful and not become too public, because what happens, or what has happened to me, is that I found myself in demand for readings. Being at the Library of Congress means that I'm really highly visible. Everybody knows that I'm there, because much was made of it when I was appointed. It was in the *Washington Post* and this paper and that paper, because I was the first Afro-American ever to hold that post. And yes, going as writer-in-residence here or a poet-in-residence there, one has to be very careful that he isn't always up before the public and not having any time at all to write poems. It gets to be very difficult, and I don't think that most poets are content to live on what they did two or three years before. I know I'm not.

I'm at the point now where I have decided to cut down on the number of readings I will give in the coming year, and to try to make myself less available for conferences and one thing or another, and to get some new work out. I intend this summer to go away, to hole myself up and not be available to anyone, and spend two or three months writing—doing nothing but writing. And next fall I will give a reading in September and then maybe another in the fall, and maybe another in the spring. But I'm going to cut down radically on the number of readings that I give, because you do reach the point where the energy that ought to go into the writing is going into public performances and so on. This can be very upsetting, because two or three years go by and you discover that you've not finished the poems that you had started before. And you just have to draw the line and not be quite so public in order to get some more work done. And yet you can't help feeling—I know I so often feel, you know, what a wonderful thing that people care enough that they ask me to come and read and they want to give me honors and so on. How lovely. Though I don't know whether I deserve it, I appreciate it and so on and so forth. But as in all things you've got to try to work out some kind of happy medium.

What are you working on now?

Well, I'm doing a series of things. I'm trying to write a long poem on Matthew Henson, the Afro-American explorer who went to the Pole with Robert Peary, and I've got four short sections of it done. And I'm working on various poems. Also

I'm trying to get a new book ready—a small book. It's going to be published in a special limited edition. I want something to come out while I'm still at the Library as Consultant.

This will be your first volume since Angle of Ascent?

Yes. I think it's going to be called *American Journal.*

Will it be all new poems?

All new poems, yes, all new poems. My regular publisher, Liveright, wanted me to wait until I had, you know, sixty or sixty-five pages. Liveright, of course, has been very good to me and very kind. I've had good luck with publishers; I don't ever fight with publishers. But my editor there felt that a book of less than, oh, fifty or sixty pages would be something that they could not handle. And so this book will be brought out by one of the small presses.

Have you done what you want to have done in terms of your work at this point?

Well, yes and no to that. I haven't done as much as I would like to do, but I think I have developed in a way that I wanted to. I think my range is fairly wide; certainly my sympathies are broad and human, you know. Nothing human is foreign to me. I do have some vision of life, some vision of the world now that I didn't have years ago. And I have more opportunities to work. I don't have to prove myself anymore. I don't have to struggle for recognition; I've got that. I still struggle to get the poems out, but that's another kind of struggle. But all in all I'd say that I'm happy for what I've done. But I'm aware that there's much more that I want to do, and there's much more that I can do. I'm hoping that I will be able within the next few years to do more work and get out some of the things that I feel are in me that I haven't been able to get out up to this point.

A "Romantic Realist"

We've been talking about the recent death of John Berryman and then more generally about the relationship between neurosis and art. Do you believe that there is a connection between the two?

No, I really don't. I don't think art grows out of neurosis. One doesn't have to be neurotic in order to be creative. When artists are neurotic I believe the reason is that the very thing that makes them creatively aware, that makes them respond to life in the particular ways they do, is also the very thing that makes them vulnerable. They're unable to throw off what I call the "burden of consciousness." And they have to make use of what hurts them. Art is not escape, but a way of finding order in chaos, a way of confronting life. I think the artist, in having to cope with the demands of life, of society (whatever *that* is), as well as with the unsparing demands of art, is often involved in ways that other people are not. An occupational hazard, one might say. A matter, also, of a certain kind of sensitivity. Or, perhaps, sensibility. One is reluctant to use the word "sensitivity," because it often connotes a sort of delicate and finespun temperament that just can't bear the realities everyone has to face. And this is not true. Most artists are

Reprinted from *Interviews with Black Writers,* edited by John O'Brien, by permission of Liveright Publishing Corporation. Copyright © 1973 by Liveright Publishing Corporation. Hayden assisted in some editing of the transcript.

tough, and if they weren't they'd never accomplish anything. Neurosis can thwart creativity. If you become too involved with the self, the ego, if you're too unhappy, you're liable to be so blocked you can't work. Hart Crane killed himself because he just couldn't cope with his problems. So did John Berryman. I suppose there's no denying, however, that sometimes art does originate in neurosis. Emily Dickinson's poems, for instance, and Sylvia Plath's. But weren't they poets *first*? Isn't such poetry an attempt to transcend neurosis—to find liberation from it through the creative act?

Are you sometimes struck by the mystery of your art?

I've always felt that poetry and the poetic process are pretty mysterious. What is it that makes one a poet? What are you doing when you write a poem? What is poetry? The feeling of mystery is no doubt intensified because you can't deliberately set out to be a poet. You can't become one by taking courses in creative writing. You are born with the gift, with a feeling for language and a certain manner of responding to life. You respond in a particular way to yourself, to the basic questions that concern all human beings—the nature of the universe, love, death, God, and so forth. And that way of responding, of coming to grips with life, determines the kind of poetry you write. Once you discover you're a poet—and you have to find out for yourself—you can study the art, learn the craft, and try to become a worthy servitor. But you can't *will* to be a poet. This is an age of overanalysis as well as overkill, and we've analyzed poetry and the poetic process to a point where analysis has become tiresome, not to say dangerous for the poet. And for all our investigations, mysteries remain. And I hope they always will.

Do you see a progression in your work? Do you realize that you are writing poetry today that you could never have succeeded with ten years ago?

I've been very much aware of that. Yes. I think I'm now

writing poems I couldn't have written ten or fifteen years ago. But I should add that some of my best-known poems were written back then. But there've been changes in outlook and technique since, and so I'm able to accomplish, when I'm lucky, what I once found too difficult to bring off successfully. I didn't know enough. Still, there are elements, characteristics in my work now, that seem always to have been present. Certain subjects, themes, persist, and—perhaps—will continue to give my work direction. My interest in history, especially Afro-American history, has been a major influence on my poetry. And I have a strong sense of the past in general, that recurs in much of my work. I don't have any nostalgia for the past, but a feeling for its relationship to the present as well as to the future. And I like to write about people. I'm more interested in people than in things or in abstractions, philosophical (so-called) ideas. In heroic and "baroque" people especially; in outsiders, pariahs, losers. And places, localities, landscapes have always been a favorite source for me. I once thought of using *People and Places* as the title for one of my books. Despite changes in outlook and technique over the years, the qualities I was striving for as a younger poet are the same ones I'm striving for today, basically. I've always wanted my poems to have something of a dramatic quality. I've always thought that a poem should have tension—dramatic and structural. And I've always been concerned with tone, with sound in relation to sense or meaning. I sometimes feel that I write by the word, not by the line. I'm perhaps oversensitive to the weight and color of words. I hear my words and lines as I write them, and if they don't sound right to me, then I know I'll have to go on revising until they do. I revise endlessly, I might add.

Did you ever fear that you might stop developing as a poet, that perhaps in another year or two years you would have exhausted yourself?

Oh, yes. A year or so ago—before I'd completed *The Night-Blooming Cereus*—I was afraid I'd never be able to write a new poem again. In the back of my mind, I suppose, I knew I would. But I didn't see how, what with all the demands on my time and energy—teaching, poetry readings, all sorts of responsibilities. I went stale, felt I was repeating myself, had nothing more to say. I've been through all this before, many times in fact. *Cereus*, which Paul Breman published, was a breakthrough for me, and no doubt that's why it's my favorite book up to now. Writing it released me, also confirmed ideas and feelings I'd had before, but distrusted. I began to move in a new direction and to consolidate my gains, such as they were.

When you first started writing, were there poets that you tried to imitate and hoped you would be as good as, some day?

When I was in college I loved Countee Cullen, Jean Toomer, Elinor Wylie, Edna St. Vincent Millay, Sara Teasdale, Langston Hughes, Carl Sandburg, Hart Crane. I read all the poetry I could get hold of, and I read without discrimination. Cullen became a favorite. I felt an affinity and wanted to write in his style. I remember that I wrote a longish poem about Africa, imitating his "Heritage." All through my undergraduate years I was pretty imitative. As I discovered poets new to me, I studied their work and tried to write as they did. I suppose all young poets do this. It's certainly one method of learning something about poetry. I reached the point, inevitably, where I didn't want to be influenced by anyone else. I tried to find my own voice, my own way of seeing. I studied with W. H. Auden in graduate school, a strategic experience in my life. I think he showed me my strengths and weaknesses as a poet in ways no one else before had done.

How do you know when a poem is completed? What tells you that it doesn't require another stanza or another image?

That's a hard question to answer. Sometimes I'm not sure, and I lay the poem aside, hoping I'll be able to come back to it with a fresher eye and ear. The time always comes, after I've written many drafts, when I know I've met the requirements, solved the problems. I feel I've realized the design. But this sense of having fulfilled my contract, so to speak, only comes after much rewriting, many, many revisions. And I must say that I rather incline to the belief that, as another poet once said, no poem is ever finished, only abandoned. There are poems, though, that I can't do anything further with. I can't get back into the mood, the frame of mind that produced them originally.

I know that your religion has greatly affected your poetry. Have your religious views changed since writing "Electrical Storm," where you recorded a near encounter with death? There seems to be a skepticism in that poem, absent in your most recent volume of poetry, Words in the Mourning Time.

No, not actually. I'm only suggesting the skepticism I might have felt earlier in my life. This wasn't a factor at the time I wrote the poem. I've always been a believer of sorts, despite periods of doubt and questioning. I've always had God-consciousness, as I call it, if not religion.

Do you think that there is a religious dimension to the work of the poet? Is there a special role that he must play in a century like ours?

Being a poet is role enough, and special enough. What else can I say? I object to strict definitions of what a poet is or should be, because they usually are thought up by people with an axe to grind—by those who care less about poetry than they do about some cause. We're living in a time when individuality is threatened by a kind of mechanizing anonymity. And by regimentation. In order to be free, you must submit to tyranny, to ideological slavery, in the name of freedom. And, obviously, this is the enemy of the artist; it stultifies anything creative. Which brings me to my own view of the role of the poet, the artist. I am convinced that if poets have any calling, function, *raison d'être* beyond the attempt to produce viable poems—and that in itself is more than enough—it is to affirm the humane, the universal, the potentially divine in the human creature. And I'm sure the artist does this best by being true to his or her own vision and to the demands of the art. This is my view; it's the conviction out of which I write. I do not set it up as an imperative for others. Poetry, all art, it seems to me is ultimately religious in the broadest sense of the term. It grows out of, reflects, illuminates our inmost selves, and so on. It doesn't have to be sectarian or denominational. There's a tendency today—more than a tendency, it's almost a conspiracy—to delimit poets, to restrict them to the political and the socially or racially conscious. To me, this indicates gross ignorance of the poet's true function as well as of the function and value of poetry as an art. With a few notable exceptions, poets have generally been on the side of justice and humanity. I can't imagine any poet worth his salt today not being aware of social evils, human needs. But I feel I have the right to deal with these matters in my own way, in terms of my own understanding of what a poet is. I resist whatever would force me into a role as politician, sociologist, or yea-sayer to current ideologies. I know who I am, and pretty much what I want to say.

There's an impersonal tone in almost all of your poetry. You're removed from what you write about, even when a poem is obviously about something that has happened to you.

Yes, I suppose it's true I have a certain detachment. I'm unwilling, even unable, to reveal myself as directly in my poems as some other poets do. Frequently, I'm writing about myself but speaking through a mask, a persona. There are troublesome things I would like to exteriorize by writing about them directly. One method for getting rid of your inner demons sometimes is to be able to call their names. I've managed to do so occasionally, but not very often. I could never write the confessional poems that Anne Sexton, Robert Lowell, John Berryman have become identified with. And perhaps I don't honestly wish to. Reticence has its aesthetic values too, you know. Still, I greatly admire the way Michael S. Harper, for example, makes poems out of personal experiences that must have been devastating for him. He's a marvelously gifted poet. I agree that poets like Harper and Lowell do us a service. They reveal aspects of their lives that tell us something about our own. One of the functions of poetry anyway. I think I tend to enter so completely into my own experiences most of the time that I have no creative energy left afterward. I'm thinking now of distressing or unpleasant experiences, obviously. And of course, everything is an experience and has meaning for me. But this is a tangential observation. To get back to the original idea, let me say that perhaps the detachment you mention is a matter of aesthetic or psychic distance. By standing back a little from the experience, by objectifying to a degree, I'm able to gain a perspective not otherwise possible. Maybe. How do I really know? Whatever I say about my poems is tentative, and certainly after the fact.

Do you think of yourself as belonging to any school of poetry? Do you place yourself in a romantic tradition as well as a symbolist?

I don't know what to say to that. I suppose I think of myself as a symbolist of a kind, and symbolism is a form of romanticism by definition. I've often considered myself a realist who distrusts so-called reality. Perhaps it all comes down to my being a "romantic realist." How would I know? Leave classification to the academicians. I do know that I'm always trying in my fumbling way to get at the truth, the reality, behind appearances, and from this has come one of my favorite themes. I want to know what things are, how they work, what a given process is, and so on. When I was writing "Zeus over Redeye," for instance, I studied the booklets I picked up at the Redstone Arsenal so I'd learn the correct terminology, get the facts about rocket missiles. I scarcely used any of this information, but it gave me a background against which my poem could move. But to return to your question: let me answer it finally by saying I hope that however I'm eventually classified, I'll still be considered a poet.

There are a few poems for which, if you recall, I would like you to describe the circumstances in which they came into being. I have tried to choose poems which might have had quite different beginnings. The first is "October."

Well, what started the poem was a long walk Erma my wife and I took through the woods one day in October. When we returned home, I jotted down a few impressions, maybe an image or two, and then several weeks later began working on the poem in earnest. October has a special meaning for me, because my daughter Maia was born on a beautiful October day. I wrote the poem as a birthday present for her, although in the early versions I didn't refer to her by name. I worked on the poem for several years, off and on. I thought it was going to be much longer than it is, but now it's more concentrated, possibly more suggestive.

And "'Lear is Gay'"?

The title is from Yeats. When I was writing this, I had in mind my wonderful old friend Betsy Graves Reyneau, who is dead now. It's dedicated to her. Betsy was an artist and a gallant human being, in many ways years and years ahead of her time. Nothing human was alien to her. She'd endured much physical suffering but had had a rich and exciting life nonetheless. She had a delightful sense of humor and could laugh at herself as well as at the world—at pretentiousness and old-fogeyism dressed up to look new. Although I was thinking mostly of Betsy, I was writing for other people too, who were old but not defeated, who weren't going to give up and retire from life, no matter how rough it became for them. And ultimately this poem is for myself. I've reached old age, and these days I hope the poem will be a sort of talisman for me.

What about "Middle Passage"?

That grew out of my interest in Afro-American history during the forties. It was to be part of a long work—a series of poems—dealing with slavery and the Civil War. I'd read Stephen Vincent Benét's poem, *John Brown's Body,* and was struck by the passage in which he says he cannot sing of the "black spear" and that a poet will appear some day who will do so. I hoped to be that poet, and I also hoped to correct the false impressions of our past, to reveal something of its heroic and human aspects. I was fascinated then, as I still am, by Civil War history, the African background, the history of slavery. I spent several years reading, in desultory research. I wrote "Middle Passage" and several other sections during the forties. But, I'm sorry to say, I never achieved my total design, owing to the fact that it was next to impossible for me to find enough time for sustained work on the book. I've discussed the composition of "Middle Passage" and other poems in the series at some length, in a book published last year, *How I Write.** Suffice it to say that "Middle Passage" was to be the opening poem in my book, which I, at first, entitled *The Black Spear,* after Benét, later, *Fire Image.* It rather amazes me to realize I wrote it nearly thirty years ago. Not much happened after it was first published, but today it's become almost a standard anthology piece.

And the poem "Those Winter Sundays"?

An intensely personal poem, one that I still react to emotionally. Written in memory of my foster father. I realized late in life, years after his death, how much he'd done for me. The poem was written during the fifties, but I can't remember how I got started on it. All I can say is that during that period I seemed to be looking back at my past, assessing my life.

Except when you are dealing with an obvious historical situation, you depend upon the present tense in your poems.

I've made a superficial—very superficial—analysis of the re-

---

*"The Poet and His Art." Reprinted on pp. 129–203.—ED.

currence of the present tense in my poems, and I think I may be using it to achieve dramatic immediacy and because in a sense there is no past, only the present. The past is also the present. The experiences I've had in the past are now a part of my mind, my subconscious, and they are there forever. They have determined the present for me; they exist in it.

There appears to be a progression in your long poem Words in the Mourning Time. *The first few sections catalogue the madness of our age, particularly that of the 1960s. Yet love enters in the last section and restores what appeared to be a hopeless condition. I'm not sure how you move from the vision of the evils to one of love. Were you suggesting that love comes after the violence and killing, or perhaps because of them?*

The final poem is the culmination, the climax of the sequence. For me, it contains the answers to the questions the preceding poems have stated or implied. If I seem to come to any conclusion about injustice, suffering, violence at all, it's in the lines about man being "permitted to be man." And it's in the last poem, written originally for a Bahá'í occasion. Bahá'u'lláh urged the absolute, inescapable necessity for human unity, the recognition of the fundamental oneness of mankind. He also prophesied that we'd go through sheer hell before we achieved anything like world unity—partly owing to our inability to love. And speaking of love, I try to make the point, in the elegy for Martin Luther King in the section we're discussing, that love is not easy. It's not a matter of sloppy sentimentality. It demands everything of you. I think it's much, much easier to hate than to love.

I wonder about the poem "Sphinx," which begins Words in the Mourning Time. *You refer to the riddle that man must answer as a "psychic joke." Could you say something about that?*

Not man, but an individual. I'm unwilling to explain the poem or the joke. Various people have come up with interesting ideas of what it is. I'll tell you this much, however: the poem revolves around the psychological, deals with some tic or block, some inner conflict you may have which gives you your particular inscape, makes you what you are. You may come, in time, to accept your condition as the definition of yourself. And the poem implies that something fundamentally negative, or apparently so, may be used in a positive, a creative way. I think that's all I need to say.

Are there poems of yours which you like very much but which have not gained attention, have not been frequently anthologized?

Oh, there are several of which that is true. The poem we've just been discussing for one. And "'Mystery Boy' Looks for Kin in Nashville" has never received the attention I feel it deserves, and there are several others I could mention. I can't complain, though. I consider most of the poems to be close to my ideal of what a good poem is, most of these have become fairly well-known and been anthologized.

Could you answer a few questions about "The Peacock Room"? What is the Peacock Room? How is the question you raise—Which is crueller?—resolved?

I find it extremely difficult to come up with coherent answers to these questions. I have complex feelings about the poem. I wanted very much to write it, felt, indeed, impelled to do so. I don't know how, quite, to put into prose statements what I struggled so hard to make the poem say. I consider it one of my most important poems; important to me, if to no one else, and to my development. And the fact that it was written in memory of Betsy Reyneau, whom I've already talked about, makes it very special to me. But let's begin with something about the Peacock Room itself. It's in the Freer Gallery at the Smithsonian, where Betsy's paintings are now exhibited. It was originally in the home of a rich English connoisseur who commissioned Whistler, the American artist, to decorate it. This was during the late nineteenth century. Whistler painted golden peacocks on the walls and doors of the room, and it therefore came to be known as the Peacock Room. It was the cause of much bitterness, even of tragedy. A younger artist had first designed the room, but the results had not satisfied the owner. Whistler undid all the work of his predecessor, and the younger artist was so appalled that he went insane. My poem, you may recall, refers to this. Whistler subsequently quarreled with his patron over his fee. There's a beautiful portrait of a young woman in the room today that Whistler painted for a Greek shipowner. It's rather exotic, Japanese. Well, that picture led to still other quarrels, because the ship-owner rejected it, and when Whistler insisted that it be hung in the Peacock Room, his patron objected. The room was dismantled after the owner's death and sold by an art dealer to Freer, a rich Detroiter and friend of Betsy's family. He had it installed in his mansion, and Betsy told me that on her twelfth birthday Mr. Freer gave a party for her in the Peacock Room. I think I'd read something about the Peacock Room but hadn't the vaguest notion of what it was like until Betsy told me about it a few years before she died. I came upon it quite by accident one day when I wandered into the Freer Gallery. Seeing it for the first time was a tremendous experience for me. I stayed there as long as I could that day, observing its details closely, my mind full of Betsy. I bought a booklet giving its history, and I got the armature of my poem partly from that account. I knew it was going to take a long time for me to write anything that even approximated the feelings I had—the sensuous enjoyment, the sadness. Perhaps the biggest difficulty—and here I'm theorizing, speaking after the fact again—perhaps the biggest problem was that I knew what I felt and I had all the background material I needed, but I didn't know how to organize, how to make a coherent whole. I learned how as I wrote. I began to see relationships. As regards the questions about art and life, let me say here that I'm aware that they are clichés, but they're still fundamental. They're archetypal. And, at my age, they're no doubt inevitable. I hope the context, the setting I've given them, redeems them, and I'm inclined to think it does. I suppose the "cruelty" of art is that it outlasts those who make it. That's simplistic, though, and doesn't begin to suggest what I mean in the poem. When I visited the Peacock Room after Betsy's death, my second and last visit, I couldn't help thinking, "Well, here are these peacocks, just as they were before, here is this room, and Betsy's dead. Whistler's dead. A whole generation's gone, but these artifacts remain." And I found myself also thinking: "What is art anyway? Why does it mean so much that it can determine one's whole life, make a person sacrifice everything for it, even drive one mad? What is it?"

How do the peacocks function in the poem?

On second and third thoughts I'd say they're necessary to convey some impression of the room, and they help to unify the poem. And, yes, they're a dramatic device, and they help to make a transition that's both emotional and thematic. They enable me to modulate from the past to the present, and from horror to serenity. The lines describing their descent "with shadow cries" and so on is rather surreal. This part of the poem cost me an agony, as Frost used to say of his poems, because what is presented there is painful to me. The peacocks lead me into this pain, and they also help me get away from it.

In "Monet's 'Waterlilies' " you refer to "the world each of us has lost." Is it a world of innocence, of childhood?

I'm absolutely cold to the voguish and overused theme of "lost innocence." Maybe I'm just too pseudo-Freudian. I might have been thinking about childhood, though surely not about innocence. But no, I can't honestly say I was even thinking about childhood. I grant you the poem could be so interpreted without doing too much violence to its meaning. Certainly, children, as we all know, live in a fantasy world, in a realm of the imagination that's forever lost to them when they grow up. But each of us has known a happier time, whether as children or as adults. Each of us has lost something that once gave the world a dimension it will never have again for us, except in memory. A botched answer, to be sure, but the best I can offer at the moment.

Is it through art that one is able to recapture it or at least become highly conscious of it?

Sometimes. That particular Monet helps me to recapture something—to remember something. I would say that one of the valuable functions of all the arts is to make us aware, to illuminate human experience, to make us more conscious, more alive. That's why they give us pleasure, even when their subjects or themes are "unpleasant."

The Poet and His Art

A Conversation

Mr. Hayden, you are a poet and a teacher. In our conversation I hope you will share the feelings and impulses that bring forth your poems. I also hope that you will discuss some of the techniques you employ. Being a poet seems, to those of us who are not poets, a strange, mystical, and probably wonderful thing. When we read a poet's works we are aware that he sees the world differently than we do. Perhaps it is that he sees more than we do. Or feels more than we do, with greater intensity. Why do you write poetry?

Because I prefer it to prose, for one thing. Because, for another, I'm driven, impelled to make patterns of words in the special ways that poetry demands. Maybe whatever it is I'm trying to communicate I can most truthfully express in poems. I think I have other reasons, too. At best, though, I can make only very tentative statements, and they're subject to change without notice. I suppose I could say, without fear of contradicting myself later, that writing poetry is one way I have of coming to grips with both inner and external realities.

From *How I Write/1*, copyright © 1972 by Harcourt Brace Jovanovich, Inc. Reprinted by permission of the publisher. Hayden's editor at Harcourt, Paul McCluskey, conducted the interview and Hayden edited the transcript. Poetry selections are reprinted from *Angle of Ascent: New and Selected Poems by Robert Hayden,* by permission of Liveright Publishing Corporation. Copyright © 1975, 1972, 1970, and 1966, by Robert Hayden.

I also think of my writing as a form of prayer—a prayer for illumination, perfection. No, I'm not satisfied with any of this. It's all beginning to sound pompous, highfalutin, but it's about as close as I can come to an answer. Most poets don't consciously analyze their reasons for being poets anyway. One doesn't choose to be a poet any more than he chooses to be born. If one could answer the question, "Why do you go on living?" then perhaps one could come up with a convincing answer to "Why do you write poetry?"

What were the earliest attempts you made to write about your feelings and experiences, and did these attempts take the form of poetry?

No. When I first began to write, I didn't write poetry. I attempted short stories and wildly melodramatic plays. As a matter of fact, I started writing when I was a child. I learned to read before entering school, and when I was in maybe the fifth or sixth grade I was trying to write stories and plays. They were imitations of movies and of plays I had seen performed by amateurs. I even tried my hand at a film script after reading some books on scenario-writing. I didn't begin to try to write poetry seriously until I was a teenager, though I vaguely recall imitating Paul Laurence Dunbar's dialect verse while still in elementary school. I well remember one summer—I was sixteen or seventeen years old—when I discovered modern poetry. I brought home from the Detroit Public Library arm-loads of books by poets like Edna St. Vincent Millay, Countee Cullen, both of whom I came to love and love even today; by Carl Sandburg, Jean Starr Untermeyer, and Orrick Johns, and other poets who are just about completely forgotten now. I read these poets and tried to write like them. And I found that I was more fascinated, more stimulated by poetry than by any other form of literature. Instead of playing baseball—I was so nearsighted I could hardly see the ball anyway the few times I played—instead of playing ball or taking part in the other so-called normal activities of the boys in my neighborhood, I would spend hours reading poetry and struggling to get my own words down on paper. From that summer on, I continued working at poetry, hoping someday to be known as a poet.

Did your early poems sound like the poems of Edna St. Vincent Millay, or Countee Cullen, or Carl Sandburg? Or did they sound like Robert Hayden?

They certainly did *not* sound like Robert Hayden. My first poems were very much like those of Edna St. Vincent Millay and Countee Cullen. Not to mention Carl Sandburg, Langston Hughes, and later, Sara Teasdale, Elinor Wylie, Stephen Vincent Benét. After reading Cullen's famous poem about Africa, "Heritage," I wrote one very much like it in theme and form. I can't remember the title now, but I do remember that it was published in a Chicago magazine, *Abbott's Monthly.* And, oh, was I proud! I must have been about eighteen at the time. Edna St. Vincent Millay—out of fashion, considered old hat today—influenced me too, as I've said. I found lines and images in her lyrics that made me want to write. And not only that. They made me look at trees, clouds, flowers, faces, as I had never looked at them before. One of the values of poetry is that it makes us aware of what we have not been aware of before. Or it may corroborate feelings we have always had, of course. But to get back to the point. I was influenced in one way or another by all the poets I read during those early years, the years of my apprenticeship. A young poet has to start somewhere, somehow. He learns by reading poets for whom he feels an affinity. But first of all, most important of all, he has to have a great love for poetry, an obsessive desire to create poems. Really, everything follows from that. He'll find his way.

As a young man, did you read the great poets of the past?

Oh, of course. Keats, Byron, Shelley, on my own; Chaucer, Burns, Wordsworth, as assignments in high school English courses. But Keats I loved more than the others. His poems seemed truly those of a young poet, with the intensity of youth, its ardor, pain, and melancholy breathing in them. Their music appealed to me, and I didn't have to understand completely what they meant in order to enjoy them. There were the marvelous images, the pictures: the moonlight shining through the stained glass window of Madeline's chamber in "The Eve of St. Agnes," the hare limping through the frozen grass, the cold statues. And there were the words and phrases like *gules, argent, cates, azure-lidded sleep,* and so on— words that chimed and glowed in my mind and set me to writing. The whole baroque atmosphere of that poem! It remains one of my favorites. I think many poets of my generation went through a Keats period. One chap I knew used to read Keats by candlelight, a kind of ritualistic act, I guess. And the fact that Keats died young had something to do with our feelings about him too, because we were all "half in love with easeful death," with the notion of writing glorious poems and dying young like Keats. And Byron meant a lot to me too, as I recall, though I didn't read much of his poetry beyond the anthology pieces and "Childe Harold's Pilgrimage." Parts of "Harold" I like because the lines were quotable and there were descriptions of exotic places. And I liked the way the poem was printed—one stanza to a page in the edition I read. But although I read the older poetry and came to love some of it enough to memorize it and try to imitate it, I was more excited by what poets in my own time were doing—such poets as I've already mentioned—and I guess I still am. I admired Carl Sandburg because he had poems with unexpected titles like "Nocturne in a Deserted Brickyard" and "To a Contemporary Bunkshooter." His diction was full of surprises for me too. He didn't use *thee* or *thou.* He made poems out of words and things that were close to the life I knew. Countee Cullen was even closer to me, because he wrote of the beauty and sadness of Negro life, which I too was aware of and wanted to express if I could. Once, I remember, I had Cullen's *Copper Sun* and *The Black Christ* with me at the welfare station. My family's caseworker saw me and was curious to know what I was reading. I showed her the books and said, "I'm going to have a volume of poems published too, someday." She smiled and went into her office. Later she became interested in me and helped me get a scholarship to college.

When you were a student, poets didn't accommodate to academic routine readily, did they? I recall that some very famous ones were expelled from college, or left of their own accord, because they couldn't adjust. How did you get along?

Well, I didn't receive the kind of encouragement I naively thought that I, as a poet, was entitled to. Not at first, anyway. One day I gave my English instructor a sheaf of what I hoped were my best poems. After a week or so he had me come to his office for a conference. Without the slightest regard for my feelings he told me that my verses were quite bad, and as if that were not withering enough, he drew a scale showing the relative positions of Shakespeare, Milton, Robinson, Frost, and Millay. "You are down here," he said, "at the very bottom of the scale." He implied that that was where my paucity of talent would undoubtedly keep me.

Were any of the poems at the bottom of that scale ever published?

No, but I had the joy of going back to my alma mater to give a poetry reading some twenty, twenty-five years later. I got over that traumatic experience. I guess I was even grateful for my instructor's harshness later on, and there's no denying that the poems were bad. But he might have let me down a bit more gently. I was, after all, a scared boy from the Detroit slums, not sure of how I'd even come as far as I had, not certain of anything except that I wanted to write poems. I was in college, of course, during the thirties, during the depression, and the motivating force behind poetry, behind most writing of this period, in fact, was social consciousness. Most of the young writers I knew were terribly earnest about changing the world, about politics, about the class struggle. We identified with the labor movement, with the so-called proletariat. We believed that our poems had to have a social message, had to preach, had to offer a solution. These were the passwords into the literary cliques of the time—*message, solution, the masses.* The Zeitgeist favored poetry that was documentary, realistic, propagandist. As young poets, we were encouraged to take as our masters revolutionary poets like Funaroff, Lola Ridge—though not the Lola Ridge of *Firehead*—Sandburg, Langston Hughes. We imitated their styles, their themes. As a fledgling poet in Detroit, I heard almost nothing of Wallace Stevens, Frost, Marianne Moore, Hart Crane. None of my friends talked of them, or if these poets were discussed, they were likely to be dismissed as bourgeois, as ivory-tower writers with no special message, as escapists. I knew nothing of Eliot or Pound when I was in college and discovered them more or less on my own years later. It's inconceivable that any undergraduate seriously interested in poetry could get through college today without knowing the work of these two poets, whose writing has been so strategic and so seminal an influence upon modern literature. But I was on my own. I'm sure there must have been contemporary literature courses, but if there were I didn't take them, probably because I wasn't an English major and therefore couldn't fit them into my program. Of course I had read a great deal of poetry, as I've indicated. But I hadn't read the difficult and experimental ones, with the exception of Hart Crane, whom I admired but whose poems baffled me. Soon after college I discovered poets like Muriel Rukeyser, W. H. Auden, Stephen Spender, Federico García Lorca.

As you read these poets, did you understand everything you were reading?

Much of it I did not understand. What was I to make of Auden's "The Orators" and "Letter to a Wound," or of his sonnet, "Sir, No Man's Enemy"? A few of the poems were completely lost on me because their references were so private as to be opaque, hermetic, and I did not like them. But there were others, particularly by Spender and C. Day Lewis, that opened up vistas for me—their trenchancy of phrase, their imagery daring, electrifying, contemporary in a manner

I had not experienced before. Muriel Rukeyser was one of the few American poets able to make powerful poems out of the events of the period. For too many others, poetry was synonymous with propaganda. "The Cause" was more important than art.

Was the influence of these poets indirect, or did you meet any of them?

I knew some of my younger contemporaries like John Malcolm Brinnin, who has become one of America's outstanding poets. We were in college together. Sometimes he would ask to see my poems, but I rarely showed him anything because I felt I didn't know as much, didn't write as well as he. I also knew Kimon Friar then, later Chad Walsh, who remains one of my most cherished friends, John Ciardi, Nelson Bentley, another beloved friend. All of them helped me in various ways, mostly by being as intense and knowledgeable about poetry as they were. Incidentally, I met Arthur Miller, the playwright, while I was a graduate student at the University of Michigan. I smile when I recall the last time I saw him; he was on his way to New York, and I wished him luck! Perhaps it would interest you to know that I took part in one of Miller's plays, *The Great Disobedience,* while at the university. I was stagestruck as a young person, acted all over the place. A few years later, I had the privilege of taking a poetry course under W. H. Auden, undoubtedly the greatest poet writing in English today. Not too long ago, I shared a poetry reading with him at Columbia University, and the occasion was, for me, almost overwhelming emotionally. I felt honored beyond all merit. But the first really famous poet I ever met was Langston Hughes. He had come to Detroit to be on hand for a performance of his play, *Drums of Haiti,* in which I played the part of a voodoo priest—a good role for a poet, I now realize, since poetry is a combination of magic, religion, mystery, incantation, among other things. I had lunch with him one afternoon and took advantage of the opportunity to show him some poems. He was interested and kind, but not terribly impressed. He told me rather frankly that although the poems had good things in them and I showed genuine talent, they were pretty conventional (as indeed they were, I'm afraid), and there wasn't much that was exciting or original in them. But he did recognize my ability, he didn't put me down, and encouraged me to keep writing. And, oh, yes, I recall that he was much taken with a sonnet I'd brought along. He laughed and said he'd never been able to write one. I told him how much I admired his poetry, told him I'd read all his books so far, and he must have seen his influence on me in the poems on ghetto life I showed him, for in those days I attempted to write of it pretty much in his style. My meeting with Hughes is one of my pleasantest recollections, for he was the first recognized poet I'd met, the first to spend time talking to me about my own poems. I came to know him rather well in the years that followed. He and my Fisk colleague, Arna Bontemps, his close friend and a distinguished writer, were the first to use my more mature work in their anthologies, and they helped me to get writing fellowships later on. I remember Hughes as an affable and engaging man, and though he undoubtedly had his bad moments like everyone else, he seemed always full of joy, full of laughter and good spirits when we were together. He had a great love of folk humor, which, as you know, comes out in his writing. And his vision of life was, as I said in another connection, affirmative. I must confess, however, that as I grew older and more concerned with matters of technique, craftsmanship, I thought less of Hughes's poetry, liked it less, than I had in the past. I felt much of it was on a level with newspaper verse, was too simplistic very often, careless in construction and development. Still, I never ceased to admire his great facility and his skill in achieving in his best poems color, tones, rhythms, imagery that were distinctly his own. And there's a "naturalness," a spontaneity, in his good poems that's certainly engaging too. Langston Hughes and I, along with Arna Bontemps, Sterling Brown, Owen Dodson, Margaret Walker, Melvin Tolson, read together on a couple of occasions at Lincoln University and Jackson College. And what stories I could tell you about these poets if there were time! Anyway, Hughes asked me to read "A Ballad of Remembrance" because it was one of his favorites. I like to remember that. When I last saw him, a year or so before his death, we were both attending the ceremony in New York at which President Leopold Senghor of Senegal presented me with the Grand Prix de la Poésie for my book *A Ballad of Remembrance,* chosen for the award at the First World Festival of Negro Arts held in Dakar the previous year. Langston came over to chat with my wife and me after the presentation and asked me to autograph my *Selected Poems* for him. I was deeply moved somehow, and I remember saying, as I tried to hold back the tears, "Well, Langston, it's a new day when you ask *me* to autograph a book for *you.*" Behind my words, you know, was the memory of that afternoon years and years ago, when I was a young hopeful with a sheaf of bad poems to show him.

That day when you lunched with Langston Hughes you were an amateur actor with some poems to show him. But had you already made up your mind at that time you were going to be *a poet?*

I think I had. I certainly was more devoted to poetry than to anything else. I cared more for it than I did for anything else. I was always reading poetry, always trying to write it. I had a friend at the public library, Marie Alice Hanson, to whom I dedicated in part my latest book *Words in the Mourning Time.* Marie Alice would put the new books of poetry aside for me, and when I kept them out beyond the due date she would sometimes pay the fines. She encouraged my love of poetry. When I began to have a few poems published she would put copies of them on the bulletin board in the poetry room of the Detroit Public Library. I was dedicated to the idea of becoming a poet, but I was not sure I had any real talent. I felt insecure about that as well as about many other things. Still, I was hoping that as time went on I would achieve some recognition as a poet. Most of my friends back in the thirties considered me a poet, and I thought of myself as one. However, I had, as I said, a good many discouragements, and I didn't know whether I was going to be a worthy servitor of the Muse or not.

What was your greatest discouragement?

Well, it's hard to say. It was probably the circumstances in which I lived. My family was uneducated, poor. But worse, much worse, than being poor—there were anyway periods when we lived fairly well—worse than the poverty were the conflicts, the quarreling, the tensions that kept us most of the time on the edge of some shrill domestic calamity. This is what the line "the chronic angers of that house" in my poem "Those Winter Sundays" refers to. We had a terrible love-hate relationship with one another, and dreadful things happened I can never forget. They turned me in upon myself, although perhaps they wouldn't have affected me so deeply if I'd not been struggling against my own inner demons, struggling with feelings of inadequacy and self-doubt. A struggle that continues to this day, I might add.

Was there a point in the writing of your poetry when you realized that you were looking back, perhaps as far back as childhood, looking at experiences from a new vantage and asking yourself if there was material there for poetry?

Oh, I always knew it was there—and in abundance—and over the years I'd attempted to write about some of my past experiences. In my first book, *Heart-Shape in the Dust,* published way back in 1940, I included a few poems reflecting my early life in Detroit. But this book was a trial flight, naturally, and the poems were 'prentice pieces. In the 1950s I seemed to look back on my childhood, my early environment, from the new vantage point you speak of. For some reason, I don't know why, I seemed to have a need to recall my past and to rid myself of the pain of so much of it. Well, perhaps the real reason why I felt this way was that during the fifties people of my generation were aware that we had reached a midpoint, and we were all no doubt constrained to look back, to see how far we'd come, maybe to see ourselves in retrospect. Whatever the reason, I began a series of poems about my life in the slums of Detroit at this time. By then I had enough detachment, I'd gained enough psychic or emotional distance to write these memory poems. I was also becoming a better poet, had a better command of technique, more insight perhaps than before.

"Summertime and the Living . . ." was written after you felt you had achieved this emotional and psychic distance?

I hadn't ever thought of this before, but it occurs to me now that writing "Summertime" was the way I achieved it, was part of the process, at least.

"Summertime and the Living . . ."

Nobody planted roses, he recalls,
but sunflowers gangled there sometimes,
tough-stalked and bold
and like the vivid children there unplanned.
There circus-poster horses curveted
in trees of heaven
above the quarrels and shattered glass,
and he was bareback rider of them all.

No roses there in summer—
oh, never roses except when people died—
and no vacations for his elders,
so harshened after each unrelenting day
that they were shouting-angry.
But summer was, they said, the poor folks' time
of year. And he remembers
how they would sit on broken steps amid

The fevered tossings of the dusk, the dark,
wafting hearsay with funeral-parlor fans
or making evening solemn by
their quietness. Feels their Mosaic eyes

upon him, though the florist roses
that only sorrow could afford
long since have bidden them Godspeed.

Oh, summer summer summertime—

Then grim street preachers shook
their tambourines and Bibles in the face
of tolerant wickedness;
then Elks parades and big splendiferous
Jack Johnson in his diamond limousine
set the ghetto burgeoning
with fantasies
of Ethiopia spreading her gorgeous wings.

You are obviously the boy speaker of this poem, yet you refer to him in the third person. Why is that, Mr. Hayden?

By writing in the third person I could be a little more objective, exteriorize up to a point. I could get a perspective and be both inside and outside of the poem at the same time. And, too, I was looking at another self—seeing myself in a different time dimension. You know the feeling you get when you see pictures of yourself as a child.

You actually depict two worlds in this poem: the world of fantasy which a boy enjoys, and the real world, which must have been harsh. I think the images for each world are strong. I'm much taken by contrasts—for example, "sunflowers gangled there sometimes" and "never roses except when people died." Would you comment on the images in the poem? Did they come readily to mind?

Most of them were down in my subconscious—that's where most of what I need for a poem is—and when I came to write "Summertime," why, they rose to the surface. Jack Johnson's "diamond limousine," for example. The sunflowers, the circus posters, and, yes, the quarrels and broken glass, even those fans, certainly came readily to mind, and writing was a part of the process of remembering them. As for the contrasts, they developed out of the material without my deliberately working toward them at first. For ghetto life as I knew it was full of contrasts. Violence and ugliness and cruelty. We kids were exposed to the grim realities, to coin a phrase, in spite of all our elders could do to protect us. But there was beauty, there was gentleness too. There was a vividness of life, an intensity of being—something I tried to suggest in the poem. And there were people who retained a—"sheltering" is the word to describe it—a sheltering spiritual beauty and dignity—my mother and my foster father among them—despite sordid and disheartening circumstances. I love the memory of those people, and "Summertime" is partly an elegy for them. The contrast between fantasy and reality, apart from the particular significance it has in this poem, is a favorite theme of mine. What is fantasy? What is reality? And can we always distinguish one from the other?

The sunflower appears rather often in your poetry, and is even used to illustrate your Selected Poems. *Is the sunflower a symbol?*

Very much so, and one I'm in imminent danger of using too often. To me, the sunflower symbolizes life, vitality, hope in the midst of deprivation. I associate it with the kind of life I knew as a young person. It was the one flower I was likely to see in my neighborhood. It grew without too much attention, I guess. I had a sunflower poem in my very first book, and maybe someday I'll revise it for my collected poems, because it has some images I still like.

Much of the effectiveness of this poem depends upon folklore.

It actually doesn't contain any folklore—not folklore as such. But we could say it reflects folk ways, aspects of folk life, attitudes. The last line, for instance, adapts a quotation from the Bible I used to hear often when people got to discussing the racial situation. "And Ethiopia shall stretch forth her hands to God" is the passage, if I remember correctly. And whatever the original meaning might have been, it had a specific meaning for us—our future glory as a God-fearing race, our freedom from oppression. "But summer was . . . the poor folks' time of year" suggests something I also heard the old folks in my neighborhood say from time to time. The street preachers I mention were in the folk tradition, with their fire-and-brimstone sermons full of horrendous imagery, their spirituals and gospel songs accompanied by tambourines. Jack Johnson was something of a folk-hero, and ghetto people admired him as a symbol of the strength and power of the black race, just as they admired Joe Louis years later. His victories were their own vicarious triumphs over the oppressor. And they saw his eventual fall as the result of a plot to destroy him because he had dared to defy the conventions of the white world.

This poem is a reminiscence. Was the act of remembering a slow process? Were there many revisions to this poem?

"Summertime," as I recall, grew out of strong emotions. I can't tell you what triggered them. A conversation with my wife about our childhood days in Detroit? An old photograph? A letter from my mother? I've forgotten what it was that quickened old memories and started me writing. At first, I was emotionally involved with my subject, but as I continued working I began to feel detached. I might very well have produced nothing but sentimental twaddle otherwise. I know we can't safely generalize about the poetic process, but I believe, from my own experience, that it's one whereby the expression of a strong emotion becomes the means of release from that emotion. Didn't T. S. Eliot say something similar? And I would say, further, that the emotion out of which a poem grows is objictified in the process of writing the poem. I wrote several versions of "Summertime" before I was satisfied with it. I'm sure that much of its effect depends on tone, pitch, and one of my problems was to keep the tone consistent. As with every poem I've written, I rewrote and revised for several years. "Summertime" was first published in *A Ballad of Remembrance,* then revised for *Selected Poems.* Everything

I originally wished to get into the poem now seems to be there, and so I think I'm through with it—at least for a while.

Can we discuss another poem of reminiscence, "Those Winter Sundays"?

Those Winter Sundays

Sundays too my father got up early
and put his clothes on in the blueblack cold,
then with cracked hands that ached
from labor in the weekday weather made
banked fires blaze. No one ever thanked him.

I'd wake and hear the cold splintering, breaking.
When the rooms were warm, he'd call,
and slowly I would rise and dress,
fearing the chronic angers of that house,

Speaking indifferently to him,
who had driven out the cold
and polished my good shoes as well.
What did I know, what did I know
of love's austere and lonely offices?

"Those Winter Sundays" is a love poem. But it is not the kind of love poem one usually reads. Here the love is that of a boy for his father, and the love seems to come only after reflection. I think it is also a sad poem, particularly in the question raised in the last two lines.

It is a sad poem, and one that I had to write, almost as an act of expiation. The last stanza—oh, it's full of regret. Many people have told me this poem expresses their own feelings exactly. Some have even wept when they've heard it at poetry readings I've given. It seems to speak to all people, as I certainly want my poems to do. For quite a while after I wrote it, I couldn't get through a public reading of this poem because of its emotional impact on me. It doesn't affect me so much now, unless I'm tired or depressed. It's in a great many anthologies, although nobody paid much attention to it at first.

Even high school youngsters like it today, which says some-thing for the poem, I should think, as well as for them. Karl Shapiro once called it a fine example of the "pure lyric."

I like another of your memory poems, "Homage to the Empress of the Blues." Who did you see, and what did you hear, to make you write this poem?

Bessie Smith, the great blues singer. She was called "The Empress of the Blues" and today all the jazz experts and black music buffs consider her to have been just that. She was close to the folk milieu, close to the soil, and she's been praised as a folk artist. Religious people—"church folks," as we used to say—thought her songs immoral, and my staunch Baptist fos-ter father, for instance, didn't want Bessie's low-down songs played on our "victorola" (victrola, that is). But we had lots of her records anyway, because my Auntie liked them. So I grew up hearing Bessie's blues. I have memories of her singing on the stage very much as I describe her in the poem. Her people loved her—with the exceptions I've mentioned—and bought her records by the thousands. The "yards of pearls" were part of an elaborate pearl costume, with tiara and all, the execu-tives of a record company gave her in appreciation for the millions of dollars her records earned for them. It's a regret-table irony that American race prejudice kept Bessie Smith from receiving the kind of recognition during her lifetime she has received since her death. And sad to recall that segre-gation, this obscene race business, was actually the cause of her death. She was in an automobile accident in the South and was refused admittance to a hospital; her life could have been saved. Bessie's blues could often make people feel hap-py-sad, a typical effect of authentic old-time blues. One of her best songs is about the Mississippi flood, "Backwater Blues." It's now considered a blues "classic," and I can image Bessie asking, "What's that?" I heard her sing it at the old Koppin Theater one night—a Detroit movie and vaudeville house patronized largely by us ghetto folks—and what a response! The clapping, shouting, whistling. She was singing about the uncertainties and sorrows of life as poor Negro people knew them—especially those who had not been out of the South very long. Here is the poem.

Homage to the Empress of the Blues

Because there was a man somewhere in a candystripe silk
    shirt,
gracile and dangerous as a jaguar and because a woman
    moaned
for him in sixty-watt gloom and mourned him Faithless
    Love
Twotiming Love Oh Love Oh Careless Aggravating Love,

    She came out on the stage in yards of pearls, emerging
        like
    a favorite scenic view, flashed her golden smile and
        sang.

Because grey laths began somewhere to show from
    underneath
torn hurdygurdy lithographs of dollfaced heaven;
and because there were those who feared alarming fists of
    snow
on the door and those who feared the riot-squad of
    statistics,

    She came out on the stage in ostrich feathers, beaded
        satin,
    and shone that smile on us and sang.

In the poems we've been discussing, particularly in this study of Bessie Smith, sound and music are important elements—lines like "Oh, summer summer summertime—" and, here, "Love Oh Love Oh Careless Aggravating Love." How important to you is the sound of your poetry?

Very important to me. I hear my lines as I write them. I'm almost as much concerned with the way my poems sound as I am with what they say. I think of the two elements interacting.

I'm sensitive to the textures, weights of words, to vowel and consonant values. I'll allow a poem to have harsh sounds—dissonances—if they contribute to the effect I'm after. Rhythm, obviously, determines tonality too. And repetition is a tonal as well as a rhetorical device. I use it more sparingly than I used to, however.

Let's talk about the sense of "Homage to the Empress of the Blues." What are you talking about when you refer to "fists of snow on the door" and when you describe "those who feared the riot-squad of statistics"?

I'm speaking of the fears and anxieties peculiar to slum life as I knew it. The insecurity. And I'm remembering through these images our cruelty to one another, the violence of the ghetto. And the menace of white authority—policemen, welfare workers, landlords. We were at their mercy, and they didn't see us as human beings. "Fists of snow" has a double meaning—the winter cold we had to protect ourselves against as best we could in our ramshackle houses; the spiritual coldness, the threat of hostile forces.

Much that we've been discussing—memories of childhood, folkloric elements, imagery—are found in your poem "Electrical Storm."

Electrical Storm
(for Arna and Alberta)

God's angry with the world again,
the grey neglected ones would say;
He don't like ugly.
Have mercy, Lord, they prayed,
seeing the lightning's
Mene Mene Tekel,
hearing the preaching thunder's deep
Upharsin.
They hunched up, contracting in corners
away from windows and the dog;
huddled under Jehovah's oldtime wrath,
trusting, afraid.

I huddled too, when a boy,
mindful of things they'd told me
God was bound to make me answer for.
But later I was colleged (as they said)
and learned it was not celestial ire
(Beware the infidels, my son)
but pressure systems,
colliding massive energies
that make a storm.
Well for us. . . .

Last night we drove
through suddenly warring weather.
Wind and lightning havocked,
berserked in wires, trees.
Fallen lines we could not see at first
lay in the yard when we reached home.
The hedge was burning in the rain.

Who knows but what
we might have crossed another sill,
had not our neighbors' warning
kept us from our door?
Who knows if it was heavenly design
or chance
(or knows if there's a difference, after all)
that brought us and our neighbors through—
though others died—
the archetypal dangers of the night?

I know what those
cowering true believers would have said.

*Certainly the circumstances that brought forth this poem are clear.
Such strong emotion comes through.*

Well, I think it's one of my most personal poems. It grew out
of an alarming experience my wife and I had one summer
night. What's in the poem actually happened, of course. Arna
Bontemps the writer and his wife Alberta were the neighbors
referred to. They lived across the street from us in Nashville

when Arna and I were on the Fisk faculty. When they heard us drive up that night they came out and called to us from their porch not to go into our house. I was just about to get out of the car, and if I had done so I would have stepped on the fallen power line. I dedicated the poem to the Bontemps to show my gratitude. Of course the poem didn't begin to take shape until quite a while afterwards, when I could look upon the experience with a certain amount of detachment, philosophical calm. After the storm abated, and the linemen had repaired the power lines that night, I stayed up until long after midnight, unable to sleep. I thought of how close Erma and I had come to being killed, or at the very least to being badly hurt. Human vulnerability—what is chance, what is accident? Is what seems chance or accident in reality part of some incomprehensible design? When I began working on "Electrical Storm," these questions became one of the most important themes in the poem.

I think we might look closely at several elements in this poem: biblical references, folklore, folk speech, and the conflict between science and religion that lies at the heart of the poem. Can we talk first about biblical allusion?

Yes. I'd like to start with the quotation from the Old Testament story of Belshazzar. *Mene Mene Tekel Upharsin*—these were the words that God wrote on King Belshazzar's palace wall, meaning "Thou art weighed in the balance and found wanting." The account of the wicked ruler is one of the great Old Testament stories I learned in Sunday School, and I use the quotation to suggest the quality of belief, the fundamentalism characteristic of the folk milieu in which I grew up. A storm was taken as a sign of God's displeasure. It symbolized his power and our helplessness. All one could do was pray to be spared, to admit one's unworthiness and ask for protection. I used to hear the older people around me, when there would be a particularly violent storm, say the words that I used in the poem, "God don't like ugly." And to that would sometimes be added, "And He cares very little for beauty."

The reference to the dog is folkloric. Superstitious people believed that animals "drew" lightning. We'd shoo our dog away from us during a bad thunderstorm so as not to be struck by lightning. I've probably given you the impression up to now that writing poetry is for me a grim rite, to be approached with fear and trembling or at least in a state of "high seriousness." Well, it is, to be sure. But it can also be fun when an old saying like "He don't like ugly" comes back to me and I find I can make use of it. Folk speech characteristically economizes, gets to the point without verbiage. Hence "colleged"—one who has been to college, and so forth. The folk elements in "Electrical Storm" are there because they are still a part of me, even though I've been "colleged" and know that dogs and cats don't "draw" lightning.

Earlier I mentioned the conflict between science and religion. Is this the central conflict of the poem?

Not to me. I think it's only suggested here. But this conflict was real enough when I was a college student. What I learned in the required science courses I muddled through—and like Thurber I never could see what was actually under that microscope!—what I learned led me to question some of the religious concepts that I had been handed. An experience shared by many of my generation. I never ceased to believe, however, for I've always had "God-consciousness," have always been something of a transcendentalist, I guess. So I didn't become an "infidel," although I must have sounded like one to my pious elders. I believed, but I believed differently.

Even in as brief a verse form as the seventeen-syllable haiku, there's conflict, or, more precisely, contrast. Is conflict or contrast a part of every poem?

Maybe not of *every* poem. But it occurs with such frequency in all types of poems that I'm tempted to say yes, categorically, though I know the dangers of generalizing. I believe that a poem should have drama, should have tension. And you get tension when there's conflict or contrast of one kind or another. There's an element of drama in a good many of my poems, because they're often based on conflict situations, often have contrasting ideas or actions.

Poems of reminiscence like the four we've been discussing are, of course, poems of experience. A young writer is nearly always advised to write first about what he knows best. What advice do you give the student poets you work with?

I too encourage them to use their own experiences, to write about what they know. But although I encourage them to look in their own hearts and write, as Sir Philip Sidney's Muse urged him to do, I am at pains to get them to see that self-expression—writing from the heart—is not all that's required. Knowledge is important. Craftsmanship is essential. And so are dedication and the willingness to work hard. For the most part, I try not to interfere too much with a young poet, once I'm convinced he's really a poet. I don't expect him to write or think as I do. And I want to let him discover some things for himself. I do demand quality, however, demand that he write better than he thinks he can. (I demand this of myself as well, I might say.) I encourage him to read as widely as possible, advise him to spend as much time writing as he can. And of course I read his poems and discuss them with him in detail. I don't theorize much, except in the most general sort of way, because I have very little patience with poetic theories. What I tell my students comes largely from my own experience as a poet, I'll say, for example, that a poem, like any other form of art, establishes its own laws and fails or succeeds in direct proportion to the poet's ability to carry them out. And I'll emphasize the point that there's always material for poetry, not lack of it, because there's poetry everywhere and in everything, waiting like the angel in the block of marble to be released.

There's poetry everywhere and poetry in everything, but everyone cannot be a poet.

Well, perhaps poets *are* born, and not made, as the familiar saying goes. To be a poet is to have a special kind of awareness, a particular quality of mind, imagination. And these can't be acquired. Everybody, though, has a feeling for poetry, however undeveloped, and maybe everyone is *potentially* a poet.

Mr. Hayden, you first visited the Deep South in 1946. Out of the South came two poems I'd like to discuss with you, "A Ballad of Remembrance" and "Tour 5." But first of all, what were your feelings, having grown up in Detroit, during this first visit to the Deep South?

Mixed, to say the very least. I found the atmosphere oppressive, terribly menacing. Although I had experienced segregation in Michigan, I was appalled by the southern brand, which I thought worse because it drew the lines between black and white so much more sharply, made everyone conscious of race in an unhealthy, a nasty way. It was obscene, dehumanizing. Nevertheless, I found New Orleans, the first big city down South I'd ever been to, fascinating. I'd read all of Lyle Saxon's books on New Orleans, and I'd heard stories about the city when I was growing up. There were people in my neighborhood who considered themselves Creoles, and they had stories to tell about voodoo and so on, and they knew how to cook Creole gumbo too. New Orleans was exotic, different from anyplace I'd seen up to that time, a foreign city. The narrow streets with French names, the palm trees (the first I'd ever seen), the famous wrought-iron balconies. I enjoyed all this as much as the racial situation, as much as my feelings of alienation and revulsion, would allow me.

In "A Ballad of Remembrance" you call New Orleans an "arcane city"—a secret, hidden city. Let's talk about the poem that grew out of the visit to New Orleans.

All right, but first of all the poem.

A Ballad of Remembrance

Quadroon mermaids, Afro angels, black saints
balanced upon the switchblades of that air
and sang. Tight streets unfolding to the eye
like fans of corrosion and elegiac lace
crackled with their singing: Shadow of time. Shadow of
   blood.

Shadow, echoed the Zulu king, dangling
from a cluster of balloons. Blood,
whined the gun-metal priestess, floating
over the courtyard where dead men diced.

What will you have? she inquired, the sallow vendeuse
of prepared tarnishes and jokes of nacre and ormolu,
what but those gleamings, oldrose graces,
manners like scented gloves? Contrived ghosts
rapped to metronome clack of lavalieres.

Contrived illuminations riding a threat
of river, masked Negroes wearing chameleon
satins gaudy now as a fortuneteller's
dream of disaster, lighted the crazy flopping
dance of love and hate among joys, rejections.

Accommodate, muttered the Zulu king,
toad on a throne of glaucous poison jewels.
Love, chimed the saints and the angels and the mermaids.
Hate, shrieked the gun-metal priestess
from her spiked bellcollar curved like a fleur-de-lis:

As well have a talon as a finger, a muzzle as a mouth,
as well have a hollow as a heart. And she pinwheeled
away in coruscations of laughter, scattering
those others before her like foil stars.

But the dance continued—now among metaphorical
doors, coffee cups floating poised
hysterias, decors of illusion; now among
mazurka dolls offering death's-heads
of cocaine roses and real violets.

Then you arrived, meditative, ironic,
richly human; and your presence was shore where I rested
released from the hoodoo of that dance, where I spoke
with my true voice again.

And therefore this is not only a ballad of remembrance
for the down-South arcane city with death
in its jaws like gold teeth and archaic cusswords;
not only a token for the troubled generous friends
held in the fists of that schizoid city like flowers,
but also, Mark Van Doren,
a poem of remembrance, a gift, a souvenir for you.

Is this a Mardi Gras poem?

No, but it contains certain details, certain images from the
Mardi Gras. The central motifs of the mask, of disguise, illu-
sion, were suggested by the Mardi Gras. And the Zulu king,
for example, has as prototype the "king" of the Zulu parade,
a parade by Negroes which used to be a feature of Mardi Gras
and perhaps still is, if the civil rights movement hasn't caused
it to be eliminated. And I hope it has. Friends in New Orleans
told me they detested the "Zulus" because they made such a
raunchy spectacle of themselves as stereotypes, outlandish
caricatures of black people. In the poem, therefore, the Zulu
king symbolizes accommodation to segregation and racial in-
justice. The saints, the angels, the mermaids, the gun-metal
priestess represent various aspects of New Orleans culture,
and you might very well find some of these figures as charac-
ters on the Mardi Gras floats that have mythical or allegorical
themes. What I did was to use elements of fantasy to point up
something by no means a fantasy, but a very grim social real-
ity. I hope, however, that "Ballad" can be read and enjoyed
without these "program notes."

In reading this poem, I'm overwhelmed by the embellishment you've given it. There are so mnay references to ornamental work—nacre (mother-of-pearl), ormolu (fake gold). The feeling I get is one of fantasy that has an almost nightmarish quality. This was done very deliberately, wasn't it?

Very deliberately, yes. My way of representing the sinister historical and social realities at the heart of the fantasy. When I thought back on my New Orleans junket, I had the impression of there being two cities. There's the one the tourist sees—the city of "prepared tarnishes," of commercialized dreams and illusions. And there is the other 'one—no less fantastic, no less dreamlike in some respects—where the racial situation is the reality and the nightmare. Both of them are in the poem. They account for the baroque quality, the ornateness of "Ballad." It's heavily embellished, as you say.

This poem makes an almost overwhelming assault on the senses: there are such strong images of color, of light and shadow, of noise. And it also contains strong images of the age, of the past, which I'm sure you chose very deliberately.

No, I rather think *they* chose *me*, in a manner of speaking. My experiences in New Orleans, though they were nothing out of the ordinary, had such a terrific impact on me, I had such an intense awareness of the cachet, the ambience, the spirit of the scene; had such a strong sense of the past within the present that I was compelled to write the poem as I wrote it. These things were inevitable. This is not to say that I wrote "Ballad" in a trancelike state! I arrived at some effects by a process of elimination.

"A Ballad of Remembrance" in a way is a kind of journey from the nightmare world to your meeting with Mark Van Doren, whose presence you describe as "shore where I rested." Tell me about Mark Van Doren.

I first met Mark Van Doren when he and I were invited to appear on a program at Xavier University in connection with a bond rally. This was just after World War II. I had read Van Doren's poetry, but I knew him by reputation only. In those days I wasn't "in" on the big stuff and wouldn't have been invited to New Orleans at all but for the fact that William Dean Pickens, at one time a rather well-known Afro-American orator and writer, knew of my work and, as a representative of the Treasury Department, sent me an invitation. Van Doren gave a talk on world peace, and I remember that he concluded with the observation that before we could ever have peace we would have to believe in the possibility of peace. After his address, I read my poem "Middle Passage," which had been recently published in an anthology. I was nervous, had stage fright, and I gave a mediocre performance. Mr. Van Doren was sympathetic when I talked with him afterwards, but he was frank enough to suggest that I learn to read my poems better. I found him to be "richly human," as I say in "Ballad," and I soon discovered that he was as outraged by the segregation in New Orleans as I was. We wanted to go and have coffee together in one of the interesting restaurants in the French Quarter, but the segregation laws made it just about impossible for us to do so. We did manage, by a ruse, to have coffee together the following day, however, and then we spent a couple of hours walking around and talking about poetry. Not long before meeting him, I'd read his latest book of poems, and I told him how much I admired him as a poet. He later sent me an autographed copy of the book. When "A Ballad of Remembrance," which is a "souvenir" for him, was published, I sent him the poem, and he wrote back that he was delighted with it. The New Orleans experience became something very special and very memorable because of Mark Van Doren. He is a great, wise, and good man. I hope the poem honors him.

Did you write this poem soon after the visit to New Orleans that occasioned it?

If I remember correctly, I wrote "Ballad" the following summer. An early version was accepted by an English magazine, but I never saw it in print, though I know it was published. I was dissatisfied with that version, and I continued working on the poem for several years. I rewrote it many times. I think I once counted fifteen different drafts.

When you began to write this poem, were you aware that it would take a kind of two-part form in which you would be released from the dance and turn to Mark Van Doren?

I'm not sure. But I knew I was going to get Van Doren into the poem by hook or crook! I'm not always sure how a poem is going to end. I used to think this was a major fault, that it meant I wasn't a very good poet, until I discovered that other poets had the same trouble. Very often when you're working on a poem, you don't know, really, you don't know all the things that are going to get into it. You don't know how you're going to work out particular problems. But as you continue writing and rewriting, you begin to see possibilities you hadn't seen before. Writing a poem is always a process of discovery. You discover things about yourself as a poet, about language, about the nature of poetry. I think it was W. H. Auden who once said to me that writing a poem is like solving for X in an equation.

Your poem "Tour 5" was also occasioned by a Southern visit, this time, I understand, to Mississippi.

Tour 5

The road winds down through autumn hills
in blazonry of farewell scarlet
and recessional gold,
past cedar groves, through static villages
whose names are all that's left
of Choctaw, Chickasaw.

We stop a moment in a town
watched over by Confederate sentinels,
buy gas and ask directions of a rawboned man
whose eyes revile us as the enemy.

Shrill gorgon silence breathes behind
his taut civility
and in the ever-tautening air,
dark for us despite its Indian summer glow.
We drive on, following the route
of highwaymen and phantoms,

Of slaves and armies.
Children, wordless and remote,
wave at us from kindling porches.
And now the land is flat for miles,
the landscape lush, metallic, flayed,
its brightness harsh as bloodstained swords.

Again, the sense of the past is strong in this poem.

Well, it could hardly be otherwise, since I'm writing about the South. In another poem I speak of the past there as being "adored and unforgiven," because it's still a part of Southern consciousness, a kind of atavistic memory. What is described in "Tour 5" is the old Natchez Trace, originally an Indian trail going from Nashville, I think, down through Mississippi and beyond. Parts of it are a highway now. Once it was a pathway through the wilderness, and it became a dangerous and sinister road used by escaped criminals, highwaymen, murderers—"the devil's highway" as I called it in a poem about the Trace I never finished.* Travelers were often robbed and killed there. It was a lurking-place for evil. But it was also used by fugitive slaves.

What were the labor pains in writing "Tour 5"?

I rewrote it several times. After the first few drafts I laid it aside because I couldn't make all the parts come together. I think in the early versions I depended too much on rhetoric,

---

*See "Theory of Evil" in *American Journal* (New York: Liveright, 1982).—Ed.

statement, not enough on suggestive images. I was overwriting as I frequently do in the first stages of a poem, trying to get too many things in. The poem got better when I cut out lines, stanzas. It's shorter now than it was at first and much more concentrated.

Why did you call it "Tour 5"?

I'm not sure now. Maybe because the route we'd taken to Jackson, Mississippi, was included in a guidebook I consulted under "Tour 5." Perhaps, also, because it's flat and prosaic in tone and thus brings an element of the unexpected to the poem. You would hardly know what the poem's about from the title, would you? Poets are forced to talk through their hats sometimes when trying to discuss their methods, and I think maybe now I'm talking through mine. Let me settle the matter by saying I probably used the title for the sake of contrast or irony.

Will I force you to talk through your hat if I ask you if you think titles are important?

Very important to me. And it's been said I have a knack for making them up. I consider the title an organic part of the poem. A suggestive title helps me to write the poem sometimes. It can set the mood, the tone for me, can help me to control content.

These two poems almost mandate a discussion of imagery. Let's start at the beginning. How do you define imagery?

The term "imagery" is used in two senses. In one, it means figurative language, figures of speech like simile, metaphor, personification, synecdoche, for instance. In the other, it denotes sensuous description, and we speak of visual, auditory, tactile, gustatory, kinetic, and olfactory imagery. This kind of imagery makes use of concrete words and phrases to convey sensory impressions. "The *glitter* of jewels," "the *hay-colored* water," "the *yellow glow* of afternoon," are examples of visual imagery. "The *booming* of the surf," "the *rustle* of the leaves," "the *shrieking* wind" suggest sounds. Images based on taste and smell are probably the hardest to manage. How do you describe the taste of apples, honey, coffee? A real challenge to a poet's ingenuity.

Of the kinds of images you've just mentioned, which do you use most often in your poems?

Visual and auditory, I should say. In "Tour 5," for example, the second and third lines contain visual images: "in blazonry of farewell scarlet / and recessional gold." Color imagery. In the third stanza there's auditory imagery—"shrill gorgon silence"—combined with kinetic: "taut civility." Most poets, I think, use visual images more often than other kinds, because sight is of such fundamental importance to us, and because to see is to experience. My own feeling for visual imagery is no doubt intensified by the fact that I'm extremely nearsighted. I've always had to make a tremendous effort to see the world clearly. As a compensation for my poor vision, I have extremely good hearing. This is sometimes a disadvantage, because I find it almost impossible to shut out sounds I don't want to hear. But it's an essential part of my "equipment" as a poet and accounts for my concern with tone, sound, cadence in my poems. My love of music contributes too.

A poet chooses an image, as a matter of fact each word, to convey a specific meaning or impression. When you read your poems to others, or discuss them with others, do you usually find that you have been successful in conveying the exact impression you had in mind?

For the most part, yes. But a poem is often a complex of meanings, of primary and secondary and even tertiary meanings. If you write with enough care and precision, the reader will no doubt get out of the poem what you originally intended. He may also find other things, and if the context justifies these discoveries, all well and good. Too often, I'm afraid, people read their own meanings into a poem, ignoring connotations, the way certain key images function, the tone. But I would say, to answer your question more specifically, that on the whole my poems seem to be interpreted correctly, with some exceptions. I have occasionally been surprised by the interpretations readers and critics have come up with.

Of the six poems we've discussed thus far, which has been most abused in interpretation?

Perhaps "A Ballad of Remembrance." I have been told it's a difficult poem. Readers frequently misinterpret the symbols, don't understand the allusions, and so forth.

If you're satisfied with "A Ballad of Remembrance" as a poetic work, does it matter what others think or say?

Well, I could say no. But that's too easy an out for the reader. Granted he thinks the poem worth his attention, I would hope he would be willing to put in some hard work and find out what's going on in it.

In presenting a difficult poem to your students, what do you do first to help them get at the poet's meaning?

That's a rather hard question to answer specifically. I think of a poem as an entity, an organic whole. The rhythm—and by "rhythm" I do not necessarily mean "meter"; I am referring to the flow, the movement of a poem—the rhythm, the images, the connotations of words, the tone, are all essential parts of the meaning. Very often students feel that when they know what a poem is about, when they've grasped the "message," the theme, they've experienced the poem. But what a poem says is really not more important than *how* it makes its statement. And the how, the method, the manner, is a very significant part of the special kind of experience a poem provides. Figures of speech, rhetorical devices, rhythm, for example, are not to be thought of as ornamentation, mere decoration; they are elements which determine meaning and serve to evoke a particular response. When working with my students on a difficult poem—one by Yeats, say—I ask them to read it several times in order to get the feel of it. Before discussing it with them, I read it aloud in class and ask them for their reactions. Do you understand what is going on? Do you like it or not? I feel it's important for them to get involved with it, whether positively or negatively. Usually, our discussion leads us into an analysis of theme, basic idea, and once we've decided what that is, we begin to consider the devices, the technique the poet has used to realize his purpose. If there are key symbols in the poem, we will study these, attempt to see how they function, how they contribute to the meaning, carry it. Sometimes, as in poems by Eliot and Cummings, the way the poem is spaced out on the page, the arrangement of the lines, even the words, are important to the meaning; and I try to make students aware of this. Of course, I think there are some poems that are rather private, that would mean one thing to the poet and something entirely different to the reader. Even so, we might enjoy them for their imagery—as is often the case with surrealistic poems— might like them for their unusual diction, their pictures, sounds.

Are any of the poems you've published hermetically sealed?

No, I don't think I have any hermetically sealed poems. But I've written some that I've consciously made rather obscure, ambiguous, because they are deeply personal, touch on aspects of my life and experience I'm not about to share with the public—directly, that is. In these poems I am rather speaking from behind the mask. I think "The Diver" in my *Selected Poems* is of this type, though it's far from obscure. On the surface—to make a bad (and unintentional) pun—it's about the experiences of a deep-sea diver, and if that's all the reader gets from it he is still responding in one of the ways I want him to. But the act of diving and the temptation the diver feels to let go, to yield to death, really represent, are symbolic of, something very personal. The entire poem is actually a metaphor.

Does the poet, by the very act of writing poetry, always put on a mask?

This is true for some poets, though obviously not for all. There are a good many today who write very directly about their experiences, who do not shrink from revealing their hang-ups, their inmost selves. This takes a certain amount of courage, a self-confidence that I for one do not have. Not that I do not try to tell the truth in my poems. I do confront my experiences and myself as honestly as I know how. I try to tell all the truth but, in Emily Dickinson's phrase, "tell it slant."

Mr. Hayden, in 1941 you addressed yourself to the task of writing a series of poems about slavery and the Civil War, a series that you had planned to gather into a collection entitled The Black Spear. *These poems are among your best-known, and I imagine that they're poems you wanted very much to write.*

Yes, indeed they are. I've always been interested in Afro-American history, and when I was a young poet, since I knew that our history had been misrepresented, I wanted to contribute toward an understanding of what our past had really been like. I set out to correct the misconceptions and to destroy some of the stereotypes and clichés which surrounded Negro history.

Specifically, how did the idea for The Black Spear *first present itself?*

Well, specifically, I became interested in writing it largely as a result of reading Stephen Vincent Benét's *John Brown's Body.* There's a passage in which he says, "O, black-skinned epic, epic with the long black spear, I cannot sing you now, having too white a heart." And he goes on to say that someday a poet will rise to sing of the black spear. I dared to hope that I might be that poet. And when I met Mr. Benét, several years after reading his book, I told him I also intended to write a poem on slavery and the Civil War, but this time from the black man's point of view. He was enthusiastic and encouraged me to do so. But I didn't begin seriously trying to write the poem, or really the series of poems, until a year or two later.

The best-known of these poems is "Middle Passage," which deals with the slave trade, partly with the Middle Passage which was the voyage across the Atlantic.

Middle Passage

I
Jesús, Estrella, Esperanza, Mercy:

Sails flashing to the wind like weapons,
sharks following the moans the fever and the dying;
horror the corposant and compass rose.

Middle Passage:
        voyage through death
                to life upon these shores.

"10 April 1800—
Blacks rebellious. Crew uneasy. Our linguist says
their moaning is a prayer for death,
ours and their own. Some try to starve themselves.
Lost three this morning leaped with crazy laughter
to the waiting sharks, sang as they went under."

Desire, Adventure, Tartar, Ann:

Standing to America, bringing home
black gold, black ivory, black seed.

        Deep in the festering hold thy father lies,
        of his bones New England pews are made,
        those are altar lights that were his eyes.

Jesus   Saviour   Pilot   Me
Over   Life's   Tempestuous   Sea

We pray that Thou wilt grant, O Lord,
safe passage to our vessels bringing
heathen souls unto Thy chastening.

Jesus   Saviour

> "8 bells. I cannot sleep, for I am sick
> with fear, but writing eases fear a little
> since still my eyes can see these words take shape
> upon the page & so I write, as one
> would turn to exorcism. 4 days scudding,
> but now the sea is calm again. Misfortune
> follows in our wake like sharks (our grinning
> tutelary gods). Which one of us
> has killed an albatross? A plague among
> our blacks—Ophthalmia: blindness—& we
> have jettisoned the blind to no avail.
> It spreads, the terrifying sickness spreads.
> Its claws have scratched sight from the Capt.'s eyes
> & there is blindness in the fo'c'sle
> & we must sail 3 weeks before we come
> to port."

> *What port awaits us, Davy Jones'*
> *or home? I've heard of slavers drifting, drifting,*
> *playthings of wind and storm and chance, their crews*
> *gone blind, the jungle hatred*
> *crawling up on deck.*

Thou   Who   Walked   On   Galilee

> "Deponent further sayeth *The Bella J*
> left the Guinea Coast
> with cargo of five hundred blacks and odd
> for the barracoons of Florida:

> "That there was hardly room 'tween-decks for half
> the sweltering cattle stowed spoon-fashion there;
> that some went mad of thirst and tore their flesh
> and sucked the blood:

"That Crew and Captain lusted with the comeliest
of the savage girls kept naked in the cabins;
that there was one they called The Guinea Rose
and they cast lots and fought to lie with her:

"That when the Bo's'n piped all hands, the flames
spreading from starboard already were beyond
control, the negroes howling and their chains
entangled with the flames:

"That the burning blacks could not be reached,
that the Crew abandoned ship,
leaving their shrieking negresses behind,
that the Captain perished drunken with the wenches:

"Further Deponent sayeth not."

Pilot   Oh   Pilot   Me

II
Aye, lad, and I have seen those factories,
Gambia, Rio Pongo, Calabar;
have watched the artful mongos baiting traps
of war wherein the victor and the vanquished

Were caught as prizes for our barracoons.
Have seen the nigger kings whose vanity
and greed turned wild black hides of Fellatah,
Mandingo, Ibo, Kru to gold for us.

And there was one—King Anthracite we named him—
fetish face beneath French parasols
of brass and orange velvet, impudent mouth
whose cups were carven skulls of enemies:

He'd honor us with drum and feast and conjo
and palm-oil-glistening wenches deft in love,
and for tin crowns that shone with paste,
red calico and German-silver trinkets

Would have the drums talk war and send
his warriors to burn the sleeping villages
and kill the sick and old and lead the young
in coffles to our factories.

Twenty years a trader, twenty years,
for there was wealth aplenty to be harvested
from those black fields, and I'd be trading still
but for the fevers melting down my bones.

III

Shuttles in the rocking loom of history,
the dark ships move, the dark ships move,
their bright ironical names
like jests of kindness on a murderer's mouth;
plough through thrashing glister toward
fata morgana's lucent melting shore,
weave toward New World littorals that are
mirage and myth and actual shore.

Voyage through death,
                              voyage whose chartings are unlove.

A charnel stench, effluvium of living death
spreads outward from the hold,
where the living and the dead, the horribly dying,
lie interlocked, lie foul with blood and excrement.

> *Deep in the festering hold thy father lies,*
> *the corpse of mercy rots with him,*
> *rats eat love's rotten gelid eyes.*
>
> *But, oh, the living look at you*
> *with human eyes whose suffering accuses you,*
> *whose hatred reaches through the swill of dark*
> *to strike you like a leper's claw.*
>
> *You cannot stare that hatred down*
> *or chain the fear that stalks the watches*
> *and breathes on you its fetid scorching breath;*
> *cannot kill the deep immortal human wish,*
> *the timeless will.*

"But for the storm that flung up barriers
of wind and wave, *The Amistad,* señores,
would have reached the port of Príncipe in two,
three days at most; but for the storm we should
have been prepared for what befell.
Swift as the puma's leap it came. There was
that interval of moonless calm filled only
with the water's and the rigging's usual sounds,
then sudden movement, blows and snarling cries
and they had fallen on us with machete
and marlinspike. It was as though the very
air, the night itself were striking us.
Exhausted by the rigors of the storm,
we were no match for them. Our men went down
before the murderous Africans. Our loyal
Celestino ran from below with gun
and lantern and I saw, before the cane-
knife's wounding flash, Cinquez,
that surly brute who calls himself a prince,
directing, urging on the ghastly work.
He hacked the poor mulatto down, and then
he turned on me. The decks were slippery
when daylight finally came. It sickens me
to think of what I saw, of how these apes
threw overboard the butchered bodies of
our men, true Christians all, like so much jetsam.

Enough, enough. The rest is quickly told:
Cinquez was forced to spare the two of us
you see to steer the ship to Africa,
and we like phantoms doomed to rove the sea
voyaged east by day and west by night,
deceiving them, hoping for rescue,
prisoners on our own vessel, till
at length we drifted to the shores of this
your land, America, where we were freed
from our unspeakable misery. Now we
demand, good sirs, the extradition of
Cinquez and his accomplices to La
Havana. And it distresses us to know
there are so many here who seem inclined

to justify the mutiny of these blacks.
We find it paradoxical indeed
that you whose wealth, whose tree of liberty
are rooted in the labor of your slaves
should suffer the august John Quincy Adams
to speak with so much passion of the right
of chattel slaves to kill their lawful masters
and with his Roman rhetoric weave a hero's
garland for Cinquez. I tell you that
we are determined to return to Cuba
with our slaves and there see justice done. Cinquez—
or let us say 'the Prince'—Cinquez shall die."

The deep immortal human wish,
the timeless will:

Cinquez its deathless primaveral image,
life that transfigures many lives.

Voyage through death
                    to life upon these shores.

"Middle Passage" obviously involved a great deal of research. How did this research begin?

It began in 1941. That year my wife and I spent the summer in New York, and while she studied at the Juilliard School, I began to do research on the slave trade, using reference material at the Schomburg Collection. I made tentative sketches for the first part of the poem, but was dissatisfied with them and soon discovered I hadn't read enough. That fall I returned to the University of Michigan to do advanced work in English, and I planned to submit a manuscript in the Hopwood creative writing competition. I hoped to have enough of *The Black Spear*, as I first entitled the series, ready to enter in the contest. I continued research on the slave trade at the University of Michigan library. I read all sorts of books, including a famous account of the slave trade entitled *Adventures of an African Slaver*. I read histories, journals, notebooks, ships' logs. Meanwhile, I was writing poems on the Civil War and poems based on folklore such as "O Daedalus, Fly Away Home," but I could not do much with the poem that was later to become "Middle Passage." I had a great deal of material, I'd taken many notes, I had gathered all the facts I needed, but I couldn't work out a form, a pattern. Actually, I had tried writing the poem in blank verse—unrhymed iambic pentameter—but, then, it was too much like Benét, not only in form, but in diction and narrative organization also. When the deadline for submission of manuscripts to the Hopwood contest came, I had finished enough of the other poems in *The Black Spear* to enter the contest. But "Middle Passage," which was to be the opening poem, was nowhere near completion. In the spring of 1942 I was awarded first prize for *The Black Spear*. I was studying with W. H. Auden at the time, and he was present when I received the award and came up afterwards and shook my hand—award enough. I continued to work intermittently on the slave trade poem during the next year or so, and gradually a form began to suggest itself.

What do you mean, "a form began to suggest itself"?

I've lost all those early worksheets, unfortunately, but I recall that at four o'clock one morning I suddenly saw how I could fit all the pieces together. I became aware of the fact that there were different voices in the poem, and this helped me to divide it into sections and achieve design and dramatic progression. From that morning on I worked to realize as fully as I could the pattern the material seemed to demand. The rhythm of the poem is basically iambic, with variations of course, and irregularities, for I wanted to avoid woodenness. The style, or method, might be thought of as, in a way, cinematic, for very often one scene ends and another begins without any obvious transitional elements. The poem is divided into three sections, and although the horrors of the slave trade are common to all, each section develops a particular aspect of this horror, focuses on a particular theme or incident.

Let's talk about these three sections.

In the opening section I describe the dreadful conditions aboard the slave ships, the brutal and inhuman treatment of the slaves. The scenes and incidents here are adapted from ships' logs, eyewitness accounts by traders, depositions. Here too I introduce the motifs, the themes, of the poem—man's cruelty to man, the Negro's heroic struggle to be free. Irony is a constant element throughout the poem. The reference to Christianity in this section, the lines from the hymn, emphasize the irony of the Christian acceptance and justification of the slave trade as a means of bringing "heathen souls" to Christ. A major irony, indeed. In the second part, we are listening to the reminiscences of an old slave-trader. And the story he tells is a composite. I took details from various accounts and combined them. The old slaver's narrative is meant to suggest a ballad, and it introduces a theme not touched on in the first part of "Middle Passage"—the complicity, the guilt, of African kings or chiefs who sold their own people into slavery. The third section is climactic. The first two move toward it. It's based on accounts of the *Amistad* mutiny, which occurred in 1839.* It's meant to recapitulate all the themes introduced earlier and focuses on the heroic resistance to slavery introduced at the very beginning.

---

*In the *Amistad* mutiny, fifty-four slaves being transported from Havana to Port Príncipe seized control of the *Amistad* under the leadership of a slave named Singbe, who had been given the Spanish name Joseph Cinquez. The captain was killed, but the two Spanish slavers aboard were spared their lives so that they could navigate the ship. The slaves demanded that the vessel sail to Africa, but at night the Spaniards would turn the vessel westward, attempting to stay close to the North American continent. Finally the ship neared Long Island and was boarded by American officials. The slaves were taken into custody and a long court battle ensued to determine whether the slaves should be charged with mutiny, or considered free men since the slave trade had been outlawed. John Quincy Adams, then a member of Congress, argued the case before the Supreme Court and the slaves were set free and returned to Sierra Leone in 1841. (Hayden's note.—ED.)

In the decisions you made which led to the final form of this poem, you obviously decided that you would employ several speakers.

Yes, there are different voices in "Middle Passage." There is the voice of the poet himself, of course, commenting on the action, the moral implications. And at times his voice seems to merge with voices from the past, voices not intended to be clearly identified. There are the voices of the traders, of the hymn-singers, and perhaps even of the dead. Yes, I would say that—the voices of the dead. In part 3, I tried to create a dramatic effect by letting one of the Spanish slavers speak. What he says in the poem is substantially what he actually said during the trial of the *Amistad* mutineers. Muriel Rukeyser's biography of Willard Gibbs, the scientist, contains a good account of the *Amistad* mutiny and subsequent trial. And the material in this section came mostly from her book.

Once you had decided upon the final form, divided the poem into parts, found various voices for the speakers, did you still do a great deal of revision?

The poem was finished in 1943 and was published in *Phylon*, then under the editorship of W. E. B. DuBois. I think it first appeared in print in 1944. After its first publication, I revised it, omitting a prologue I had written earlier but found I didn't need. The poem was next published in Edwin Seaver's *Cross Section: 1945* and subsequently revised again. I dropped whole stanzas as well as lines and phrases I thought wrong or imprecise. I revised the poem again for the collection of my poems Paul Breman published in London in 1962. Since that time I've done no more work on it, although I intend some day to revise the ending.

You're not satisfied with the ending?

No, I would like to change it somewhat, make it stronger. I have the feeling now there's something more I should say in order to round the poem off.

Shakespeare's The Tempest *obviously came to your mind as you wrote this poem. This may be a good point to talk about allusion.*

"Deep in the festering hold thy father lies, / of his bones New England pews are made, / those are altar lights that were his eyes." These lines echo Shakespeare's song from *The Tempest*: "Full fathom five thy father lies; / Of his bones are coral made; / Those are pearls that were his eyes." I hoped my lines would set up reverberations in the minds of readers familiar with Shakespeare's. And I was perhaps attempting to establish an ironic relationship between his use of the themes of death and metamorphosis in the song and my own. Looking back, I suppose I felt there was some connection between the sea change he describes and the change from human beings into things, objects, suffered by enslaved Africans. This, and the idea that slavery was a kind of death. I can't give a better explanation than this, I'm afraid. After all, I wrote "Middle Passage" more than twenty years ago, my original drafts are lost, and I can't remember in detail everything that went into its creation.

The hymn "Jesus Saviour Pilot Me" appears almost as a refrain. And it appears in a rather startling way on the printed page. Would you comment on this?

The spacing of the lines throughout the poem is for dramatic effect. It serves as a means of transition from one episode or theme to another. And it's therefore essential to the meaning, to the emotional impact. The hymn obviously suggests false piety, Christian guilt and hypocrisy. I spaced the lines of it so they would register as counterpoint, as ironic commentary perhaps. And, further, the hymn helps to unify this section, perhaps even to slow it down. It's spaced the way it is to give emphasis to an important theme in this part of the poem. But let me say in all honesty that I wasn't deliberate about everything I did in this poem. I just felt some things were right, would have dramatic impact, and would increase the sense of irony I was hoping to convey.

Teachers and students so often take a poem like this apart line by line, always asking, "Why did the poet do this? Why did the poet do that?" Your answer suggests to me that sometimes the poet doesn't know, that sometimes the poem just grows.

Yes and no to that. A poem, and this one I think would certainly be a good example of what I have in mind, is a fusion of the conscious and the unconscious, the deliberate and the mysterious, the imaginative and the rational. As I worked on "Middle Passage," I knew there were certain things I wanted to do, ideas I wanted to present in as dramatic a way as I could, but I couldn't be deliberate about everything, couldn't really plan beyond a certain point. Some things evolved as I wrote, some things I consciously tried to get into the poem, and some elements appeared unexpectedly, rather like spontaneous combustion, but really were the result of all the reading and thinking I had done beforehand.

Were you angry when you wrote "Middle Passage"?

No, I wasn't angry. But, again, I was emotionally, psychologically involved with the poem. I wanted to be the one who'd fulfill Benét's prophecy—wanted to write the poem he confessed he couldn't write. And since I was aware of how our history had been distorted, I aimed to write a poem that would give the lie to the bigots. But I wanted it to be a *poem* and not vindictive rhetoric, not propaganda.

May we turn now to your poem "O Daedalus, Fly Away Home"? I know about one Daedalus, the Daedalus who with his son, Icarus, flew from the Cretan labyrinth using artificial wings made of wax and feathers. Daedalus escaped to Sicily, while Icarus flew too near the sun and fell into the sea when his wings melted. Your Daedalus lives in the Georgia pines. Is he the same Daedalus?

Yes, he's the same in the sense that he represents the same human longing for freedom, for the lost homeland. I tried to suggest this in the title, which combines classical allusion with a line from a spiritual. The poem is actually based on a legend common among the Georgia Sea Island Negroes—the legend of the Flying African. It was believed there were certain Africans who, after being brought here as slaves, flew back to Africa. They had magic power, and, as I say in the poem, they could just spread their arms and fly away. Reading versions of this legend as told by ex-slaves, I was struck by the fact that fundamentally it was pretty much the same as the story of Daedalus and Icarus.

Let's turn to this poem which grew out of legend and myth.

O Daedalus, Fly Away Home
(for Maia and Julie)

Drifting night in the Georgia pines,
coonskin drum and jubilee banjo.
    Pretty Malinda, dance with me.

Night is juba, night is conjo.
    Pretty Malinda, dance with me.

Night is an African juju man
weaving a wish and a weariness together
    to make two wings.

    O fly away home fly away

Do you remember Africa?

    O cleave the air fly away home

My gran, he flew back to Africa,
just spread his arms and
    flew away home.

Drifting night in the windy pines;
night is a laughing, night is a longing.
    Pretty Malinda, come to me.

Night is a mourning juju man
weaving a wish and a weariness together
to make two wings.

O fly away home fly away

This poem is developed contrapuntally. Sadness and nostalgia counterpoint gaiety and dancing. "Daedalus," incidentally, has been performed as a dance poem. The rhythm is accentuated—most of the lines are trochaic—in order to suggest movement, dancing. I slow it up in places, shifting the accent from the first syllable to the second, and so on.

A juba *is a dance. What is a* juju?

Juju has to do with magic. It's an African word. A *juju* man would be a conjurer, a magician.

"The Ballad of Nat Turner" is another of your best-known poems. Can we talk about it?

The Ballad of Nat Turner

Then fled, O brethren, the wicked juba
        and wandered wandered far
from curfew joys in the Dismal's night.
        Fool of St. Elmo's fire

In scary night I wandered, praying,
        Lord God my harshener,
speak to me now or let me die;
        speak, Lord, to this mourner.

And came at length to livid trees
        where Ibo warriors
hung shadowless, turning in wind
        that moaned like Africa,

Their belltongue bodies dead, their eyes
    alive with the anger deep
in my own heart. Is this the sign,
    the sign forepromised me?

The spirits vanished. Afraid and lonely
    I wandered on in blackness.
Speak to me now or let me die.
    Die, whispered the blackness.

And wild things gasped and scuffled in
    the night; seething shapes
of evil frolicked upon the air.
    I reeled with fear, I prayed.

Sudden brightness clove the preying
    darkness, brightness that was
itself a golden darkness, brightness
    so bright that it was darkness.

And there were angels, their faces hidden
    from me, angels at war
with one another, angels in dazzling
    combat. And oh the splendor,

The fearful splendor of that warring.
    Hide me, I cried to rock and bramble.
Hide me, the rock, the bramble cried. . . .
    How tell you of that holy battle?

The shock of wing on wing and sword
    on sword was the tumult of
a taken city burning. I cannot
    say how long they strove,

For the wheel in a turning wheel which is time
    in eternity had ceased
its whirling, and owl and moccasin,
    panther and nameless beast

And I were held like creatures fixed
        in flaming, in fiery amber.
But I saw I saw oh many of
        those mighty beings waver,

Waver and fall, go streaking down
        into swamp water, and the water
hissed and steamed and bubbled and locked
        shuddering shuddering over

The fallen and soon was motionless.
        Then that massive light
began a-folding slowly in
        upon itself, and I

Beheld the conqueror faces and, lo,
        they were like mine, I saw
they were like mine and in joy and terror
        wept, praising praising Jehovah.

Oh praised my honer, harshener
        till a sleep came over me,
a sleep heavy as death. And when
        I awoke at last free

And purified, I rose and prayed
        and returned after a time
to the blazing fields, to the humbleness.
        And bided my time.

Nat Turner led a slave-revolt in Jerusalem, Virginia, in 1831.
It did not succeed, as we know, but it was one of many such
blows for freedom which helped to weaken the Southern
slavocracy. As I studied accounts of the rebellion, what in-
terested me was not the bloodshed but Nat Turner himself,
his characteristics, his personality. He was a quiet, deeply re-
ligious man—a preacher, in fact—a strange, lonely, "other-
worldly" man. He brooded, he kept away from others, would

have considered "wicked" the frolicking described in "Daedalus." I read somewhere that he was never known to smile, never laughed. And he actually had the vision of the warring angels. Details like these, and Turner's essentially mysterious qualities, greatly stimulated my imagination. I came to see him as a gothic figure, as a rather frightening kind of vengeful mystic whose faith in the Old Testament God of battles was absolute.

In this poem you speak to the reader in the persona of Nat Turner. How does a poet get "inside" another person?

Well, I don't know that I really got "inside" Nat Turner. I read a great deal about him, and then I let my imagination have full play over the facts I'd gathered. In the ballad I imagine him talking to his followers, preparatory to the revolt. By having him speak, I thought I could reveal him more dramatically and with greater economy. I could create a stronger illusion of a living presence.

There's been so much concern of late with charismatic figures. Do you think Nat Turner was a charismatic man?

Oh, I'm positive he was. He was a man with a mission, and he attracted followers who believed in him and his visions.

You frequently include "The Ballad of Nat Turner" in your poetry readings. How is it received?

It's a poem people seem to like, and nobody has attacked it yet as being untrue to history. But you know, William Styron's *Confessions of Nat Turner* became a storm center when it was published a few years ago, because there were those who thought the author deliberately misrepresented Nat Turner—emasculated him. Styron's motives were questioned, were indeed condemned as racist. And a group of writers brought out a volume denouncing him. My ballad, by the way, was written several years before Styron's book appeared—was written, interestingly enough, long before the revival of interest in this figure. So far, I haven't been accused and brought to trial for what I wrote. And at this point, I would like to say for the record that the attack on Styron, the extremely harsh criticism leveled against him, should give all writers pause. We have reason to be alarmed. Are we to be restricted in our choice of subjects? It's true that Afro-American history has been traduced. And it's true that as a people we have been stereotyped and caricatured in literature almost beyond recognition. And we're therefore hypersensitive. But even if Styron's book were as gross a misinterpretation as some people consider it, would chauvinistic censorship be the proper remedy?

What advice would you give a young poet who's going to attempt a poem of this kind, a poem in which he chooses a figure from history to write about?

I'm afraid I have nothing but truisms to offer. And one of them is that he should read as much as possible about his subject, learn as much about the historical background as he can. You have to do your homework, study your character so closely that what you imagine him saying or doing is undergirded by the facts you've gathered—has, therefore, plausibility. Looking at pictures helps too. I very often study old prints, illustrations in books, old posters, photographs. I've spent hours and hours going through such books as Mathew Brady's volumes of Civil War Photographs. This kind of research helps me to visualize my characters and their setting, gives me a feeling for the period in which they lived. Visiting historical museums may be a help too. The spiked bell-collar in "A Ballad of Remembrance," for instance, is a device I saw in the Cabildo in New Orleans. It's a pronged iron collar with bells on it that slaves were forced to wear as a punishment for having attempted to escape. An appalling instrument of torture. Once having seen this thing, I never forgot it, and it became a symbolic image in my poem. As for "Nat Turner," I read various accounts of his revolt and books on slave-lore and plantation life, among them *The Negro in Virginia*. And so by the time I started writing, I had stored up facts and images that were there when I needed them. I want to emphasize the point, however, that although the facts, the background information, are important—important as armature, scaffolding—it's not the facts per se that make the poem. Or even get you started writing it. It's what the imagination does with the facts. It is, moreover, the poet's attitude, his vision, his emotional response to the material that lead to the poem. And, finally, I think one has to be careful not to permit his biases to distort the material he has set out to use. Truth—at least as much truth as one is capable of discerning and expressing—and accuracy are desirable goals.

"Runagate Runagate" is also from this collection.

Runagate Runagate

I.

Runs falls rises stumbles on from darkness into darkness
and the darkness thicketed with shapes of terror
and the hunters pursuing and the hounds pursuing
and the night cold and the night long and the river
to cross and the jack-muh-lanterns beckoning beckoning
and blackness ahead and when shall I reach that somewhere
morning and keep on going and never turn back and keep
  on going

      Runagate
          Runagate
              Runagate

Many thousands rise and go
many thousands crossing over
            O mythic North
          O star-shaped yonder Bible city

Some go weeping and some rejoicing
some in coffins and some in carriages
some in silks and some in shackles

      Rise and go or fare you well

No more auction block for me
no more driver's lash for me

> If you see my Pompey, 30 yrs of age,
> new breeches, plain stockings, negro shoes;
> if you see my Anna, likely young mulatto
> branded E on the right cheek, R on the left,
> catch them if you can and notify subscriber.
> Catch them if you can, but it won't be easy.
> They'll dart underground when you try to catch them,
> plunge into quicksand, whirlpools, mazes,
> turn into scorpions when you try to catch them.

And before I'll be a slave
I'll be buried in my grave

> North star and bonanza gold
> I'm bound for the freedom, freedom-bound
> and oh Susyanna don't you cry for me

Runagate
　　Runagate

II.
Rises from their anguish and their power,

Harriet Tubman,

woman of earth, whipscarred,
a summoning, a shining

Mean to be free

And this was the way of it, brethren brethren,
way we journeyed from Can't to Can.
Moon so bright and no place to hide,
the cry up and the patterollers riding,
hound dogs belling in bladed air.
And fear starts a-murbling, Never make it,
we'll never make it. *Hush that now,*
and she's turned upon us, levelled pistol
glinting in the moonlight:

Dead folks can't jaybird-talk, she says;
you keep on going now or die, she says.

Wanted   Harriet Tubman   alias The General
alias Moses   Stealer of Slaves

In league with Garrison   Alcott   Emerson
Garrett   Douglass   Thoreau   John Brown

Armed and known to be Dangerous

Wanted   Reward   Dead or Alive

Tell me, Ezekiel, oh tell me do you see
mailed Jehovah coming to deliver me?

Hoot-owl calling in the ghosted air,
five times calling to the hants in the air.
Shadow of a face in the scary leaves,
shadow of a voice in the talking leaves:

Come ride-a my train

Oh that train, ghost-story train
through swamp and savanna movering movering,
over trestles of dew, through caves of the wish,
Midnight Special on a sabre track movering movering,
first stop Mercy and the last Hallelujah.

Come ride-a my train

Mean mean mean to be free.

What does the title mean, Mr. Hayden?

Runagate is an archaic form of *runaway*. An old word used to
describe a fugitive, a runaway slave.

Was this poem inspired by the posters which advertised rewards for the
return of runaway slaves?

Part of it was, I would say. But I got the idea for the poem largely as a result of reading about the Underground Railroad and Harriet Tubman, one of its most fearless and spectacular agents. Harriet escaped from slavery, then led hundreds—some accounts say more than three hundred—of slaves to the North and Canada before the Civil War. Many years ago I wrote a play about her, a very bad play titled *Go Down, Moses.* It was just as bad as it could be, though I do feel today that what it lacked in dramatic technique it made up for in spirit and melodramatic daring. Even this bad play couldn't kill my interest in Harriet Tubman, however. She was so dramatic a figure and had become so real to me that I still wanted to do something with all the exciting material I had gathered but hadn't known how to use in the play. I can't recall when it was I first began to work on "Runagate." But it may be of interest to you to know that after an early version of the present poem had been published I thought it was as bad as the play and put it aside. Several years later, it was published, without my knowledge, in England. And when Rosey Pool came over from London to visit Fisk—this must have been in the early sixties—she gave a program of readings from American Negro poets, and among the things she read was "Runagate Runagate." Now I hadn't dared look at this poem for years, and as Rosey read it I was amazed and gratified to discover that most of it was much better than I'd thought. And as Rosey read—she is one of the finest readers of poetry I've ever heard—I realized the poem was worth saving, worth working on some more. Rosey Pool, by the way, is a brilliant Dutch woman who lives in London and has edited several anthologies of Afro-American poetry. I told her later what her reading had done for the poem. I went back to "Runagate," revised it drastically, though I kept the form I had used in the other versions.

The train in the poem is, of course, the Underground Railroad.

Yes—the Underground Railroad, which was imaginary, a metaphor. When I read about it as a young person I thought there had actually been subterranean passageways or tunnels or something. But the Underground Railroad was a railroad only in the sense that there were well-defined routes from the South to the North which fugitive slaves and their guides used. And it was underground in the sense that the methods of escape and the activities of those connected with the railroad were kept secret as far as possible, were shrouded in mystery. Then too, escaping slaves usually traveled at night, and night has always been associated with mystery, with the unknown.

Rhythm is an important element in "Runagate Runagate," is it not?

Indeed it is. In the opening strophe the lines move rapidly, and there are no pauses between words, phrases. I've not used punctuation, and I've sort of run everything together because I'm trying to suggest the flight, the breathless flight, of the anonymous fugitive who is meant to typify, to represent, the courage and desperation and determination of all those thousands of fugitives who fled from slavery. I try to suggest movement in other sections of the poem too. I rewrote and rewrote until I got exactly the effect I wanted. I wanted a number of things to be going on simultaneously.

This poem is also very melodic.

That's partly due to the rhythm, partly to the use of lines from spirituals. In some places I've repeated lines and phrases, and this repetition also contributes to the music of the poem. But on the whole I think it's the beat, the rhythm, that gives it this quality.

In all of the poems we've discussed, I've very rarely seen rhyme. Do you avoid rhyme?

Maybe not intentionally, but I seem not to use it much any more, not even to want to use it. I have written rhymed poems, but the effects I'm after now I seem to achieve without rhyme. My forms are always rather free anyway, and rhyme tends to be somewhat confining. And perhaps it smacks too much of the conventions of the past. I don't know. Don't be surprised if in my next book you find poems with elaborate rhyme schemes. Rhyme can be a way, after all, of exerting control over the material.

Let's turn to a poem which has a more conventional form, the sonnet "Frederick Douglass."

Frederick Douglass

When it is finally ours, this freedom, this liberty, this
     beautiful
and terrible thing, needful to man as air,
usable as earth; when it belongs at last to all,
when it is truly instinct, brain matter, diastole, systole,
reflex action; when it is finally won; when it is more
than the gaudy mumbo jumbo of politicians:
this man, this Douglass, this former slave, this Negro
beaten to his knees, exiled, visioning a world
where none is lonely, none hunted, alien,
this man, superb in love and logic, this man
shall be remembered. Oh, not with statues' rhetoric,
not with legends and poems and wreaths of bronze alone,
but with the lives grown out of his life, the lives
fleshing his dream of the beautiful, needful thing.

Why did you choose this form for "Frederick Douglass"?

Originally I had intended to write a sonnet sequence for *The Black Spear* dealing with several of the outstanding figures in the antislavery struggle, and "Douglass" was to be the culminating, the climactic poem in the series. I wrote five or six of these, and Louis O. Martin, who published my first book in Detroit in 1940, printed them in a short-lived magazine of his. The sonnet on Douglass was the only one I liked, and so in time I discarded the others. This sonnet owes something to Gerard Manley Hopkins, the late-Victorian poet. He altered the sonnet form, pushed it beyond conventional limits, made it freer than it had been before. I doubt very much if his poem, "That Nature is a Heraclitean Fire," would be recognizable at first as a sonnet, in terms of its structure, unless you knew his prosodic system, his highly individual—rather eccentric—style. Hopkins abandoned iambic pentameter as the norm for the sonnet line—although he occasionally made use of this rhythm—and employed a pattern of stresses or accents. As he worked it out, this meant that there might be any number of syllables in a line but only five or six would be accented. Well, when I was working on my own sonnets I was also studying Hopkins, and under his influence I decided to experiment with stressed verse. I thought this would make for the kind of intensity I was after. I succeeded, more or less, in adapting Hopkins's technique to my own purposes, though I don't feel I imitated him any more than Dylan Thomas or Auden did when they too employed aspects of his technique in their own poems. "Douglass," then, is not in iambic pentameter. Certain words in each line receive accent, and there are usually five stresses in each line. Though it doesn't rhyme, as sonnets are supposed to, it does contain the required fourteen lines.

The rhetoric of "Frederick Douglass" seems more elevated than the poems we've been discussing.

I agree with you. "Frederick Douglass" was written at a time when I was consciously striving, I now realize, for "grand" effects. It was to be part of my projected *magnum opus,* remember. I still like this sonnet and think it stands up very well, even though it was written more than twenty years ago, when I was not only struggling to learn my craft, to acquire my own signature, but also agonizing over the (to me) life-and-death question of whether I was a poet or not. Anyhow, it's one of the most widely anthologized of all my pieces, having been "discovered" in recent years. I suppose I would write it quite differently today, though perhaps I couldn't write it so well. Douglass was an extraordinary man, a genius, a hero in every sense of the word. When I undertook to write about him, I wanted to avoid hollow praise rhetoric; I wanted to make a serious statement expressing his greatness, his historical and spiritual significance. And I wanted loftiness of tone, because the subject clearly demanded it. All this sounds terrible today, because we associate "loftiness" with inflated rhetoric and are suspicious of the heroic. I confess I share these feelings, for the most part. But to get back to the poem we're talking about. I was also trying to get down to something fundamental, universal, and so I used words like *diastole, systole,* and I tried to make my imagery suggest what was basic, elemental, enduring. The poem is tightly constructed, taut and wound up like a spring. It doesn't let go of the reader until he comes to the final line. Or so it seems to me now each time I read it before an audience.

All of these poems were to be part of a collection, The Black Spear. *We have the poems, but we don't have* The Black Spear. *What happened?*

I abandoned the work eventually. But not before I had completed it, more or less, and sent it around to various publishers. A few editors thought it had possibilities, but most of them thought parts of it were better than the whole. And they were right. You see, by the time I'd come to the end of it, *The Black Spear* was a mixture of styles, idioms. One reason for this was that during the years I worked on the series—and I must have been at it, off and on, for at least seven—my outlook, my style, my technique, were changing. Another reason was that during all that time I'd been teaching, first at the University of Michigan and afterwards at Fisk University, and I almost never had time for really sustained work. I had to write whenever I could find a few hours after everything else was done. And of course there were other difficulties too. I had energy and enough stamina, though, not to let circumstances defeat me entirely. I did finish *The Black Spear* and write poems such as "Ballad of Remembrance" as well. But *The Black Spear* in its final form was fragmented, a mixture. I was able to salvage the best of the poems I'd written for it, but I lost interest in the project as I'd planned it originally. Obviously, I didn't lose interest in writing history poems, for "Runagate" and "Nat Turner," for example, were written afterwards. And "The Dream" in my latest book, *Words in the Mourning Time,* combines two of the poems I had written for the series a long time ago. Perhaps some day I will gather all my history pieces and publish them in one volume, and what started out as *The Black Spear* will have a different sort of organization and a new title but will be essentially the book I first tried to write many, many years ago.

In 1954–55, you received a Ford Foundation grant which enabled you to travel, study, and write in Mexico. When you went to Mexico were you consciously looking for material for poems?

I suppose every poet, every artist, when he visits another country hopes to replenish his resources, hopes to find material his imagination can make use of. But if he's too methodical, too deliberate in his quest for "material," he may not find anything, because he can't "see for looking," as the old phrase goes. It seems to me you don't choose your material anyway; as some other poet once said, it chooses you. When I went to Mexico I hoped I would be stimulated to write, yes. I had a collection of poems in manuscript I wanted to finish while there, and I hoped the change of scene and the leisure to "loaf and invite the soul" would help me get the kinks out of my psyche so that I could revise my poems and get them ready for publication. But I went to Mexico primarily because I wanted to experience another culture. I was a Spanish major in college, and I've always been intensely interested in Latin America, in everything Spanish. I didn't expect to be able to write about Mexico while in the country. I can hardly ever make poems about anything I'm involved in at the moment. I have to wait until I'm able to get a perspective on it, until I can sort of objectify, exteriorize my experience. I must confess I did try to force a lyric or two out of hiding, but I didn't produce anything of consequence. I kept a notebook, jotting down details I wanted to remember, and I sketched out poems I didn't complete until after I'd returned home.

Do you think there's a point at which every writer must find some spiritual refreshment and replenishment?

I would say this is true for everyone, not just for writers.

I'd like to talk about one of the poems that came out of your stay in Mexico, a poem whose title you'll have to translate for me—"Sub Specie Aeternitatis."

The title means "under the aspect of eternity" and comes from a Latin phrase used by the philosopher Spinoza. The poem is one I wrote after visiting a convent in Tepotzlán. Tepotzlán is a little Mexican town much studied by anthropologists because the people there, descendants of the Aztecs, of course, have retained ancient customs and beliefs that were common before the conquest of Mexico by the Spaniards. Here, as in other parts of Mexico, the old gods are still present. The town itself is rather picturesque—a word we use with caution today—and lies at the foot of the mountains. A group of us drove out there from Mexico City one Sunday afternoon to see an old Dominican convent dating back a couple of centuries, if I remember correctly. It's empty now, but in good condition. During the Mexican revolution, convents and monasteries were closed by the government, and they remain closed to this day. Now they're "tourist attractions," nothing more. So much for the background of "Sub Specie Aeternitatis." Now here's the poem.

Sub Specie Aeternitatis

> High amid
> gothic rocks the altar stands
> that honored once
> > a tippling fiercely joyous god.
> > Far below,
> the empty convent lifts
> its cross against a dark
> > invasive as the sun
> > whose plangent fire
> moves like feathered snakes
> in trees that shade
> > the cloister-garth.

                    The curious
          may walk the cloister now,
          may enter portals barred
                    to them no longer
                    and wander
          hidden passageways and rooms
          of stone, meditating on
                    such gods as they possess,
                    as they have lost.

                    Hollow cells
          are desolate in their
          tranquility
                    as relic skulls.
                    Arched windows there
          look toward the firegreen mountain
          resonant with silence of
                    a conquered and
                    defiant god.

Here again, the sense of the coming together of past and present is so strong, reminding one of your poem set in New Orleans, "A Ballad of Remembrance." Yet this whole thing is certainly more than a matter of geography.

Undoubtedly. Perhaps it can be attributed to my strong sense of history. And to my feeling for irony and contrast—two elements that recur in my poetry. I seem always to be aware of the past within the present. And I know that in regard to my own life, I am often painfully conscious of how my experiences as a young person shaped—misshaped?—me, determined my present. Some of them were terrible, I assure you, but I guess they gave me the strength, the toughness I needed to survive as a poet, if not as a "well-adjusted" individual. And so they were, as Isaiah says, "treasures of darkness." But I'm getting off the subject. In Mexico the impact of the past is everywhere dramatically apparent, and it accounts for some pretty startling contrasts. You will see Indian vendors in regional dress selling birds in the Paseo de la Reforma, Mexico

City's most elegant boulevard. Modern buildings, almost futuristic in design, will have mosaic murals—fantastic, kaleidoscopic—depicting scenes from Mexican history or simply blazing with Aztec symbols, Aztec iconography. The national cathedral is built on the site of an Aztec temple—actually over the ruins of it. There are the great pyramids of the sun and the moon built centuries ago. And the faces of the people often remind you of old Aztec masks. The Mexican past seemed remarkably viable to me, gave Mexico its special kind of ambience.

We haven't talked much about form. When you begin to write a poem, do you think about form, or does a form suggest itself as you set your thoughts down?

I would answer yes to both parts of the question. I always hope, as I've said before, that there's going to be a close relationship between form and content. Occasionally, I will have a definite pattern in mind before I begin writing. This was true of the Douglass sonnet. If I'm in luck, if the Muse is not too recalcitrant, I can manage. (Note the "if's"; writing poetry, let's face it, is an "iffy," sometime thing!) Usually, though, I have to try a variety of forms and methods before I arrive at something that seems right. That's why each poem is for me an experiment. At the beginning, I'm not always sure of what the "shape of the content"—to borrow from Ben Shahn—is going to be. And I don't know how a poem is going to end much of the time. A pattern begins to emerge, very often, as I write, and it affects the meaning. Once I see the pattern clearly, I let it guide me. "Sub Specie Aeternitatis," I recall, was hard to organize. It didn't succeed when it was freer, more "open" than it subsequently became. It just didn't work at all. It was loose, needed considerable tightening. In the early drafts the lines were arranged differently. Some were short, and some were longer than they are now. Eventually, the varying lengths of the lines suggested a stanza pattern I was able to work with, and then the poem began to, well, began to be a real poem.

You told me earlier that you hear your poems. Does hearing them help you to determine their form?

I suppose it does, in a general sort of way. I've not thought much about it, actually. What I can say definitely is that I'm concerned with phrasing, with cadences, pauses, with tone. And these certainly contribute to the structure as well as to the meaning of my poems. Maybe this is as good a place as any to say something I feel is rather important, and that is: a poem should have silences. For me the silences of a poem are as meaningful as its sounds. All my best poems have silences in them. There are things in them that are not expressed, that are all the more strongly suggested because they are not stated.

Let's talk now about one of your thinnest poems, "Market." Of course I'm not trying to speak here as a critic but simply as someone looking at the poem as it appears on the printed page.

Market

Ragged boys
lift sweets, haggle
for acid-green
and bloody gelatins.
A broken smile
dandles its weedy
cigarette
over papayas too ripe
and pyramids
of rotting oranges.
Turkeys like feather-
duster flowers
lie trussed in bunchy smother.
The barefoot cripple
foraging crawls
among rinds, orts,
chewed butts, trampled
peony droppings—

his hunger litany
and suppliant before
altars of mamey,
pineapple, mango.
Turistas pass.
Por caridad, por caridad.
Lord, how they stride
on the hard good legs
money has made them.
Ay! you creatures
who have walked
on seas of money all
your foreign lives!
Por caridad.
Odor of a dripping
carcass moans
beneath the hot
fragrance of carnations,
cool scent of lilies.
Starveling dogs
hover in the reek
of frying; ashy feet
(the twistfoot beggar laughs)
kick at them in vain.
Aloft, the Fire King's
flashing mask of tin
looks down with eyes
of sunstruck glass.

Certainly, as the title of the poem tells us, it is partly a description of a marketplace and of people you've seen there. I suspect it's more than that, though.

It is. But, again, I find it hard to explain it in a prose statement. I wanted, clearly, to describe the market, with its color, its activity, its exotic atmosphere, its squalor. Yet I was after more than the merely picturesque. The market scene focuses impressions, certain feelings I had about Mexico—the harshness of existence for the poor, the indifference, or seeming indifference, to human misery I so often encountered there, the cruelty and beauty inherited from the past. The beggar in the poem unifies these, pulls the whole poem together so that it's a little drama, not simply description.

How does a scene such as the one you describe in "Market" come to you? Is it one remembered image—that is, photographic like a single picture, or is it a composite of many things you saw?

I was thinking mostly of the large indoor market in Mexico City I went to a few times. But I also used images remembered from other markets I visited in Toluca, Puebla, Pátzcuaro. The things I describe might have been found in any of them. The crippled beggar, the boys, the dogs came readily to mind, since they are so much a part of any market scene in Mexico. The situation in the poem is imaginary—the encounter between the beggar and the tourists, I mean.

A word about the diction of this poem, particularly the few Spanish phrases. Could you talk about that?

I used them to give a touch of "local color" to the poem. For flavoring, you might say. I used to hear beggars in the streets saying, *"Por caridad, señor, por caridad"*—"Have charity," it means; "for the sake of charity," literally. A characteristic phrase. Perhaps it also functions in the poem as a means of suggesting the barrier between the tourists and the cripple, lack of communication.

In the poem you mention the tourists and you make a rather hard comment when you say, "Lord, how they stride / on the hard good legs / money has made them." Here you are looking at the market from the point of view of the beggar.

Well, more exactly, these are meant to be the beggar's own thoughts, not mine. I'm not necessarily putting the *turistas* down but suggesting the beggar's attitude. I could imagine him contrasting his miserable condition with the tourists' well-being, resenting these people for their apparent affluence while hoping to arouse their pity and thus get a coin or two out of them.

A final question about "Market." In all of your Mexican poems there are such strong images of the sun, particularly here in the last four lines. Would you comment on the imagery here?

The imagery of the last four lines is based on a rather elaborate tin mask I bought at the Mexico City market. It's big and shiny, with glass eyes that glow when the light strikes them. It's wonderfully barbaric in appearance. The vendor told me it represented the Fire King, and perhaps he meant by that a sun deity; I've never found out. At any rate, it's Indian in origin and design, and it seemed a fitting symbolic image with which to close the poem. It can be interpreted as representing the dead, yet living, past of the Mexican Indian and the powerlessness of the old gods to help him.

A third poem from this collection is simply entitled "Kid."

Kid
(Cuernavaca)

He is found with the homeless dogs
    that worry sidewalk cafes
where gringos in dollar bills
    deplore and sip. He has

Tricks of pathos for
    the silly foreigners
and so manages not to starve.
    Waiters strike at him and curse;

Deft and quick and accustomed,
    he dances beyond their blows,
taunts them and scampers off,
    laughing as he goes.

Was there a certain child in a certain place that brought about this poem?

Yes—a little boy I used to see in Cuernavaca. Cuernavaca is a favorite of tourists and of artists and writers—a charming town where there are some overpowering murals by Diego Rivera as well as the beautiful Borda gardens created for the Empress Carlotta in the nineteenth century. I went to Cuernavaca a few times while in Mexico, and I would spend leisurely hours at one of the sidewalk cafés, drinking coffee and reading or scribbling down my observations of the scene in the hope of future poems. And this *chamaco*—"kid" in English—would usually be around, begging for coins or sweets. The waiters would drive him away, and he would skedaddle, laughing and cussing a blue streak, as the saying goes. Very often as he ran past the tables he'd snatch the *pan dulce*—sweet roll—off your plate if you weren't on guard or stick a finger in the sugar bowl. The whole caper was a game he never tired of playing. He'd return, after being chased away, and start the performance all over again. I occasionally gave him a coin to get rid of him. He couldn't have been more than seven or eight years old, and he was ragged, dirty, and had tetters. I gathered he had no home, or perhaps had left it to fend for himself, sleeping in doorways or on the sidewalks at night, like far too many other Mexican waifs and strays. He was already a toughie, was already smoking cigarettes. But although he was a pest, I felt sorry for him, seeing how bright and clever he was, knowing he had no future, except perhaps as a criminal. He came vividly to mind when I was writing my "Mexican sheaf," and I would have felt the series was incomplete without a poem about him. As it stands today, "Kid" is the final version of a much longer poem in which I attempted to suggest the boy's background and felt impelled to make some kind of social comment. But I found the long poem didn't come off, since there were irrelevant details in it and it tended to become didactic. All I needed to say is now in the poem as I finally revised it. I regret, though, that in the process of rewriting I omitted some details. But to have kept them would have made the poem loose and maybe rhetorical.

Is there often a temptation for the poet to take the pulpit or to argue for social causes?

There is for me, quite often. And never more so than now in this "late, bad time," as the critic Nathan Scott has characterized the period we're living in. I have my causes. I am not "above the battle." I feel very strongly about the war in Vietnam and the racial struggle, and I've written poems about them. But as a poet, I hope, not as a pseudo-politician and certainly not as the *spokesman* for a cause.

Did you feel, as you sat in the sidewalk café, like a gringo, *a foreigner?*

Let me begin with my favorite paradox, my favorite personal cliché: No place is home for me, therefore every place is home. Yes, I sometimes felt very much the *gringo*, the outsider. But not too often, actually, perhaps because I speak Spanish and had no trouble communicating with people. They could see I was interested in the country, sympathetic. I visited several towns and cities in Mexico, talked with all sorts of people. In Vera Cruz, for instance, the Indian caretaker of an old fort I went to see asked me if I were an Aztec! Imagine! That was one up for my Spanish. When I laughed and told him I was an American Negro, he didn't know what I meant by *Negro*. And, of course, who really does? But let's get away from controversial topics. I lived with a Spanish family in Mexico City and came to feel very close to them. Mapi, the señora whom I called *la reina de la casa*—"the queen of the house"—used to address me as "my son"—*hijo mío*. She was a great soul, a humanitarian if ever I knew one, and she also loved off-color jokes and popular sayings, and so I learned from her what I had never learned in college Spanish. By living as I did, I came to understand many things about the country and the people. Still, the culture *was* different, and there were attitudes and practices that I as an American found distressing, had to get used to. Being a Bahá'í kept me from feeling as much a stranger as I might otherwise have. For I came to know several Mexican Bahá'ís, was invited to their homes, made trips with them. The faith we shared diminished our superficial differences, was a bond between us.

You went to Mexico to travel, study, and write. Where would you like to go next?

(Laughs.) Oh, I'd say almost anywhere, but I would certainly like to go to Europe. And the American Southwest—Arizona, New Mexico. All over the world, really, to see as many different kinds of people, cultures, as possible.

How is a poem born? From our discussion it seems that it is a slow process. Sometimes it involves the remembrance of things past, sometimes it is sparked by a single incident or experience, and sometimes a poem comes together as a kind of collage of experiences. Some poems, such as "Middle Passage," have grown out of long study and research. We've talked about all these kinds of poetry in our examination of your work, Mr. Hayden. To conclude our conversation, I've chosen three poems—"Full Moon," "Zeus Over Redeye," and "Monet's 'Waterlilies'"—three poems which all seem to convey strong personal feelings: your religious beliefs, your view of today's technology coupled with your sense of the past, and your love of art. Let's turn first to "Full Moon." Was this poem written to commemorate the conquest of the moon in 1969?

It was written several years before the astronauts reached the moon. I'd been reading magazine articles about the moon, browsing through books on rocketry at odd moments, but not with the intention of writing anything. This must have been in the early sixties. There's a version of this poem in Rosey Pool's *Beyond the Blues* and Herbert Hill's *Soon, One Morning,* published in '62 and '63 respectively. And since I rarely let go of a poem until I've worked on it for a year, at least, this means I must have written it in 1960 or '61. My friends laugh when I tell them I went out on the porch one summer night and looked up and saw the moon, then rushed back to my study and began writing. They laugh, but that's just about the way the poem came about. It was as though I'd seen a full moon for the very first time. I am fairly certain I'd had no conscious intention of writing on the subject. Indeed, all the talk about the military importance of the moon had rather put me off. Also, I was hardly enthusiastic over the prospect of technology storming one of the last bastions of fantasy. I don't feel that way today, however. I see new possibilities for poetry in the discoveries that have been made. Lunar actualities appeal to my imagination as much as lunar fantasies, maybe more.

Full Moon

No longer throne of a goddess to whom we pray,
no longer the bubble house of childhood's
tumbling Mother Goose man,

The emphatic moon ascends—
the brilliant challenger of rocket experts,
the white hope of communications men.

Some I love who are dead
were watchers of the moon and knew its lore;
planted seeds, trimmed their hair,

Pierced their ears for gold hoop earrings
as it waxed or waned.
It shines tonight upon their graves.

And burned in the garden of Gethsemane,
its light made holy by the dazzling tears
with which it mingled.

And spread its radiance on the exile's path
of Him who was The Glorious One,
its light made holy by His holiness.

Already a mooted goal and tomorrow perhaps
an arms base, a livid sector,
the full moon dominates the dark.

"Full Moon" has a definite chronology. Would you trace it stanza by stanza?

The poem moves backwards and forwards in time. In the first stanza there are negative references to myth and fantasy from the past. In the second stanza we are in the present, the technological present. In the third and fourth stanzas we are in the past again, but now it is the poet's own personal past. The mood, the tone here, I feel, are rather elegiac. We move farther back in time in the fifth stanza to the night of Christ's agony in the garden. From there we move to the nineteenth century—to a spring night in 1863, to be specific. "The Glorious One" alluded to is Bahá'u'lláh, prophet of the Bahá'í Faith, and like Christ a divine manifestation. Both are seen in a moment of crisis. In the final stanza we come back to the present, which seems full of foreboding. The dark referred to in the last line is both the darkness of night and the darkness of the age and our future prospects.

The reference to the Bahá'í Faith in this poem is one of many that appear in your poetry. How important are your religious beliefs to you as a poet?

As a Bahá'í I am committed to belief in the fundamental oneness of all races, the essential oneness of mankind, to the vision of world unity. And these are increasingly powerful influences on my poetry today.

"Zeus Over Redeye" is another poem in which you look at the present and speculate somewhat about the future.

Zeus over Redeye
(The Redstone Arsenal)

Enclave where new mythologies
of power come to birth—
where coralled energy and power breed
like prized man-eating animals.
Like dragon, hydra, basilisk.

Radar corollas and Holland tulips
the colors of Easter eggs
form vistas for the ironist.
Where elm, ailanthus, redbud grew
parabola and gantry rise.

In soaring stasis rocket missiles loom,
the cherished weapons named for Nike
(O headless armless Victory),
for Zeus, Apollo, Hercules—
eponyms of redeyed fury
greater, lesser than their own.

Ignorant outlander, mere civilian,
not sure always of what it is
I see, I walk with you among
these totems of our fire-breathing age,
question and question you,

who are at home in terra guarded like
a sacred phallic grove.
Your partial answers reassure
me less than they appall.
I feel as though invisible fuses were

burning all around us burning all
around us. Heat-quiverings twitch
danger's hypersensitive skin.
The very sunlight here seems flammable.
And shadows give
us no relieving shade.

I'm told that this poem always draws strong response in your poetry readings.

It does. I'm sure audiences respond to it because most of us today are appalled by the potentialities for mass death and destruction our society has created. We feel insecure, not protected, feel threatened by what can be described as the technology of disaster.

This poem was obviously written after you made a visit to the Redstone Arsenal.

I went out there one spring morning several years ago with a member of the staff. My reactions to what I saw, my feelings, were pretty much as they are stated in the poem. I could scarcely say any more about the experience now without repeating what I think I've said much better in the poem.

Did the writing of "Zeus Over Redeye" present any particular challenge to you?

It did, to be sure. And I was glad for the challenge. A poem that comes easily, I have found, is usually not worth bothering with. And this one was hard to write, because there were aspects of the subject I didn't clearly understand. I had to learn something about rocket missiles, although I didn't use the information directly. The challenge was to write on a subject I knew little about and was therefore afraid to tackle. Yes, the challenge was to write this poem at all.

I think the poem well meets that challenge. Let's talk now about "Monet's 'Waterlilies.'"

Monet's "Waterlilies"
(for Bill and Sonja)

Today as the news from Selma and Saigon
poisons the air like fallout,
        I come again to see
the serene great picture that I love
and flames disfigured once
        and efficient evil may yet destroy.

Here space and time exist in light
the eye like the eye of faith believes.
        The seen, the known
dissolve in iridescence, become
illusive flesh of light
        that was not, was, forever is.

O light beheld as through refracting tears.
Here is the aura of that world
        each of us has lost.
Here is the shadow of its joy.

Would you describe Monet's "serene great picture"?

I've described it in the poem about as well as I can. It's iridescent, full of light and shadow. Monet, you recall, was said to paint with light. It's one of several in his series of waterlily paintings. It used to hang by itself at the Museum of Modern Art, but now it's part of a tryptich, and I wish it weren't, because the canvases on each side of it are in dark tones of green and blue and to my eye they detract from its delicacy.

You say of the painting, "flames disfigured once." Did that actually happen?

Oh, yes. There was a fire at the Museum several years ago, and this painting was partly burned and had to be restored. It's a great blessing it wasn't destroyed.

In the final stanza of the poem, what do you mean when you say, "Here is the aura of that world each of us has lost"?

That's just this side of being sentimental, don't you think? But it's the way the painting makes me feel. It suggests to me a past that is gone and will never come again. It's from another world. From another time, in an emotional, a spiritual sense. The life, the quality of mind and spirit that produced French Impressionism are gone and will never come back. And there's something more personal: When I look at this Monet I have a feeling of nostalgia. It reminds me of some place I've never been to, yet is familiar to me and is in a way a home I've lost. I know this doesn't make any sense, but that's the effect the painting has on me. I hasten to add, however, that I love the painting not because I can "program" it, so to speak. I respond to its colors—they're like sounds—to the sheer visual delight it gives.

Mr. Hayden, it is nearly a cliché to say that Robert Hayden has the best underground reputation of any poet in America. How do you respond to that?

(Laughs.) I say Hear! Hear!

UNDER DISCUSSION
Donald Hall, General Editor

Volumes in the Under Discussion series collect reviews and essays about individual poets. The series is concerned with contemporary American and English poets about whom the consensus has not yet been formed and the final vote has not been taken. Titles in the series include:

Elizabeth Bishop and Her Art
edited by Lloyd Schwartz and Sybil P. Estess
Richard Wilbur's Creation *edited and with an Introduction by Wendy Salinger*
Reading Adrienne Rich *edited by Jane Roberta Cooper*

Forthcoming volumes will examine the work of Robert Bly and Allen Ginsberg, among others.

Please write for further information on available editions and current prices.

Ann Arbor   **The University of Michigan Press**